D1716314

African Literature Today

An annual review
Edited by Eldred Durosimi Jones
Number 5: The Novel in Africa

HEINEMANN
London · Ibadan · Nairobi · Lusaka

AFRICANA PUBLISHING CORPORATION
New York

Heinemann Educational Books Ltd
48 Charles Street London W1X 8AH
P.M.B. 5205 Ibadan · P.O. Box 45314 Nairobi
P.O. Box 3966 Lusaka
EDINBURGH   MELBOURNE   AUCKLAND   TORONTO
HONG KONG   SINGAPORE   KUALA LUMPUR
KINGSTON   NEW DELHI
ISBN 0 435 91655 6
© Heinemann Educational Books Ltd
First published 1971
Reprinted 1973, 1975, 1977

Published in the United States of America 1971
by Africana Publishing Corporation
a Division of Holmes & Meier Publishers, Inc.
101 Fifth Avenue
New York NY 10003
All rights reserved
Library of Congress Card No 702505
ISBN 0 8419 0094-9

All articles and editorial correspondence to
Professor Eldred Durosimi Jones
Department of English
Fourah Bay College
University of Sierra Leone
Freetown
Sierra Leone
It is regretted that unsolicited manuscripts
cannot be returned unless the authors provide
return postage

Printed in Great Britain by
Morrison & Gibb Ltd
London and Edinburgh

Contents

Editorial

From this number, *African Literature Today* changes from a twice-annual to a once-yearly publication. This change, it must be admitted, threatens the liveliness of such dialogue as the journal may stimulate. To keep critical exchanges from going stale, the editor plans to invite comments and replies, where these seem warranted, in good enough time for both an original view and reactions to it to appear side by side.

Once the value of criticism is conceded the author can be no less entitled to talk about his work than the most perceptive critic. Even the creator, though, becomes limited by what appears on the page, and what can be legitimately deduced from it. If authors and critics can come together within these limits of debate, the results could be reciprocally valuable.

To make up for the longer gaps between numbers, *African Literature Today* will be larger. This number is devoted mainly, though not exclusively, to articles on the novel. The next number will be principally devoted to poetry. It is planned that future numbers will each feature some special aspect of African Literature.

Eldred Durosimi Jones

ARTICLES

African literature: What does it take to be its critic?

Ernest Emenyonu

African literature has come to mean several things to several people. To some it is a tool for the literate African's arrogation of the essence of his cultural heritage – an assertion and at times an imposition of the contents and excellence of a black culture, on a white dominated world. To others African literature means 'a new literature of the world' with its authentic and original genre, themes, and message. To a few, it is simply a political document of protest against the assumptions of colonialism and imperialism as they relate to the world of the black man. To yet other people, African literature in all its ramifications represents a mere appendage to British or French literature since most of the African writers write chiefly in English or French.

It would appear that the literary world was not prepared for the emergence of African writing when it did. Those who posed as its 'judges' knew little or nothing of the existence and depth of oral literature in Africa, and therefore, little or nothing of the true roots of written African literature. Some of them were gaining their first insight into the African social scene, and approached African writing for its sociological rather than its literary interest. Criticism of African literature, **1** therefore, centred around the discovery of the degree of new information on African primitive ways which each subsequent work revealed.

Some of these people were quick to rush to the conclusion that they would soon get bored with the content of African writing. When Chinua Achebe's second novel *No Longer at Ease* appeared in 1961, many critics had no further doubts in their minds that the African novel of the second half of the twentieth century was simply the sociological document that they suspected it of being from the start. When *Arrow of God* (Achebe's third novel) emerged, this conclusion became absolute. But when further works from African pens (including Achebe's) came out with emphasis on other things apart from 'primitive' social idiosyncracies of remote Africa, the critics' dilemma and unpreparedness showed in their approach to the works. In the Western world some universities quickly dichotomised African literature into the traditional, meaning oral, and the modern, meaning written. Critics had little to say about the former because as Dr Edris Makward has pointed out: 'Literary criticism as a separate and autonomous specialty or genre had no place in pre-colonial Africa, where the best qualified and reliable critics were indeed the public itself.'[1] In spite of this, however, some teachers have still engaged in the task – helped by two or less years of graduate study in an African language – of translating African folk tales and assigning their students to read the printed word and 'discover' the qualities of a good African folk-tale.

The critics of the so-called 'modern' African literature became more confused in their purpose and approach than some college departments who wanted to see in African literature a steady source for the ethnographic data of the 'old Africa rediscovered'. Some of them only began then to do what they should have done from the beginning – recognise that the novel is a Western form, and therefore, concern themselves with what the African novelists 'have done to their derived form instead of the amount of traditional ritual and modern rottenness and rheum that is to be found in them'.[2]

Some did not see this exercise as worth anything because a novel by an African in the English or French language must in the final analysis have nothing noble enough to recommend its form. A British critic did not equivocate in a London newspaper when he said:

We are in for a spate of 'quaint' books from Africa written in what almost amounted to 'pidgin English' – this is the new writing of Africa and the only true way in which the African can speak his mind and convey his emotions and environment in the English language.[3]

2

But the non-'quaint' books from Africa sounded too good to have their sources in Africa. So critics began to find godfathers for the successful or popular African writers. If a book became successful then it must be because the author had an as-yet-undiscovered root in a Western literary tradition, or had all his life been reading the works and philosophies of great Western literary figures, and this is the discovery that the critic made. If it was unsuccessful or it contained the looked-for fetish, then, of course, it became truly African.

In a loosely written book entitled *African English Literature*, Anne Tibble, not satisfied with finding in Amos Tutuola's *Palm Wine Drinkard* episodes which reminded her of 'the money-changers whipped from the Temple' by Jesus, or the 'story of Gomorrah', and 'the Flood in reverse', concluded that Tutuola's:

> mixing of modern wonders, radios, telephones, guns, and bombers, with Crusoe-Anderson-Treasure Island gnomes, imps, goblins, cudgels, cutlasses, and jungles, openly states his debt to previous tale-tellers. Clearly he has read a great deal of non-African folk and fairy tale. But his mixture of ancient and modern is an added part of his fascination for the young.[4]

Anybody who knows anything about Amos Tutuola's literary background knows that it is misleading to suggest that Tutuola 'clearly has read a great deal of non-African folk and fairy tale' before writing *The Palm Wine Drinkard*. The same is true of Tutuola's 'mixing of ancient and modern'. If one is able to see African literature as a cohesive piece of study which is made more interesting by the changes that it undergoes in its complexion and emphasis as a result of the cultural, historical and social circumstances which act on its existence, then such things as the 'mixing of ancient and modern' would not be difficult to explain. As Okogbule Wonodi pointed out:

> Folk tales are elastic and progressive changes in the modes of behaviour and values are continually filtering into age-old tales . . .
> Age-old stories about oppressed orphans now have the added injustice of the orphans not being sent to school. The moneys used in the tales are no longer cowries but pounds, shillings, and pennies, but by the end of the story, we are back in our familiar world of present-day Nigerian coinage.[5]

It is not because Wonodi is African that he is able to know this. If Anne Tibble had looked to African (indeed Yoruba) oral literature as Tutuola's source and not 'non-African folk and fairy tales' perhaps she could have come to such a simple deduction. Compare Anne Tibble's **3** discussion with E. N. Obiechina's in *Presence Africaine*, No. 65, 1968. But Anne Tibble is not alone in this search for the roots of African literature initiatives outside Africa. Because Chinua Achebe derived the title of his first novel from a poem by W. B. Yeats, Miss A. G. Stock has recently written an article showing the connection between the theme of Achebe's novel and Yeats' vision of history 'as a succession of civilisations, each giving way to another through its own inability to embrace all human impulses satisfactorily within one closed order.'[6] Having made her point, Miss Stock then tries to make token appreciation of Achebe's literary abilities as an original writer within the 'African' context! What can one argue against this case – that *Things Fall Apart* is not the story of Umuofia society (or African civilisation for that matter) giving way to the Western civilisation because of the former's inability to embrace all the indigenous and foreign human impulses satisfactorily within one closed order? Or is one (besides Achebe himself) to argue that Achebe has never been a disciple of Yeats in thought or deed, which is the 'discovery' that Miss Stock has made.

In the same way, J. P. Clark is said to echo the Greek visions of tragedy and reminds many people of T. S. Eliot. Other established African writers possess declared and undeclared 'godfathers' while the emerging ones are waiting to have the critics announce their forebears. It is indeed surprising that no one has made any 'discovery' yet about the connection between African writers and the big grandfathers in American, German, Russian, and Chinese fiction. Would it not be worthwhile for instance 'discovering' how much Wole Soyinka owes to Neil Simon or Peter Abrahams to Leroi Jones and James Baldwin?

Recently Bernth Lindfors made a towering discovery of the source of Cyprian Ekwensi's literary inspiration. In an article entitled 'Cyprian Ekwensi – An African Popular Novelist', published in *African Literature Today*, No. 3, 1969, Lindfors concludes with: 'All this said, Ekwensi's novels are still failures. They combine some of the worst features of Western popular literature with some of the least subtle techniques of African oral narrative art. It seems that when Ekwensi is not trying to get by with cheap effects borrowed from shoddy sources, he is labouring to make an obvious point. Thus, rather like his heroes, he vacillates between complete Westernisation and reversions to his African heritage. There would be nothing wrong with mixed foreign and native narrative traditions in a literary work, if it were artfully done. But Ekwensi lacks artistic discretion, and for a popular novelist there is no more fatal flaw.'

In analysing Lindfors' article in detail, it can be shown what inadequate information can do to mislead even well-intentioned minds.

Lindfors started off by declaring that Ekwensi is a perfect example of where 'practice does not make perfect' and not one of all Ekwensi's novels, novelettes, folk tales and short stories 'is entirely free of amateurish blots and blunders, not one could be called the handiwork of a careful, skilled craftsman'. Lindfors intended to use this to raise the eyebrows of the reader by his impending discovery. 'Unlike other African writers', Lindfors declares, 'who address themselves to Europe or to an educated African elite, Ekwensi prides himself on being a writer for the masses, a writer who can communicate with any African literate in English.' Though Lindfors has been too hasty in deciding the audience for all African writers except Ekwensi, it must be pointed out that Ekwensi has no particular audience in mind black or white, except the reader who 'enjoys stories of incident and character'. He does not need to be inside Africa to qualify for this.

To use his own expression, it seems that 'not one of Lindfors' conclusions on Ekwensi's art is entirely free from amateurish blots and blunders'. He asserts that Ekwensi 'obtained most of his stimulation from third-rate American movies and fourth-rate British and American paperback novels'. He further asserts that 'these are certainly the most pronounced influences on what Ekwensi has written'. That there have been influences on Ekwensi's (as in any other writers') writings is incontestable, but they are not the type that Lindfors thinks.

One can say that Ekwensi is unique among his contemporaries. An Ibo from Nkwelle near Onitsha, Eastern Nigeria, Cyprian Ekwensi was born at Minna in Northern Nigeria, and he passed his childhood days in the Hausa culture. He came down to Western Nigeria for his high school education and thus spent his adolescent days in the Yoruba culture where he later on taught. Later he went to Achimota College in Ghana (then the Gold Coast) and finally to London, England for further studies in pharmacy. His career details show that Ekwensi started off as a forestry officer, then a teacher of biology and chemistry (and later pharmaceutics), then a chemist and druggist, next a pharmacist, then Head of Features in the Nigerian Broadcasting Corporation. Later on Ekwensi became Director of Information Services, Chairman, Bureau for External Publicity and then Controller-General, Broadcasting Corporation of the former Republic of Biafra.

This is important because it is the stage of life and consequently the environment of each period of his career that has been the chief influence on whatever Cyprian Ekwensi has written. These influences on his works can be divided very roughly as follows: 1. Childhood in Northern Nigeria: *Passport of Mallam Ilia; An African Nights Entertainment*; 2. High School in Western Nigeria, plus later teaching in Western **5**

Nigeria: *Drummer Boy; Rainmaker and Other Stories; Trouble in Form Six;* 3. Life as a Forestry Officer: *Burning Grass; The Leopard's Claw; Juju Rock;* 4. Life in Lagos (as student, as teacher, as pharmacist): *When Love Whispers; People of the City; Jagua Nana; Iska; Yaba Round-about Murder; Lokotown and Other Stories;* 5. War in Nigeria: *Afri-chaos* (an unpublished MS.) The folk tales fall under the general influence of his Biafran origins, his parents, being themselves very good storytellers. If Lindfors knew all these he would not it is hoped, have tried to prove something about the gap between Ekwensi's publication dates and the actual dates when the author wrote the works. Ekwensi is known to keep diaries of events in his life, and he decides at what time to articulate any such records into creative fiction.

Lindfors was making a mountain out of a molehill when he tried to make some conclusions from the novels that Ekwensi had read and was thrilled by in his school days – Rider Haggard, Edgar Wallace, Dickens, Sapper, Bates. Lindfors does not seem to know that any other West African who went through the unfortunately British dominated educational system read virtually the same titles as Ekwensi. The only thing that should be known about Ekwensi in this regard is that he had an early overpowering and almost compulsive interest in reading, especially fiction. So possessed was Ekwensi by this trait that even while his reachers were solving mathematical equations on the blackboard, Ekwensi was preoccupied with novels hidden between his legs beneath the desk. The strange thing is that even in such books as *Passport of Mallam Ilia* and *Burning Grass* with all their pastoral setting and language, the only thing that succeeds in coming across to Lindfors is the huge debt they owe to the 'Wild West' stories. In the same way that Anne Tibble 'discovered' that Tutuola 'had read a great deal of non-African folk and fairy tales', Lindfors also 'revealed' that 'Ekwensi was apparently familiar with all the standard clichés of the western'.

Perhaps the oddest assertion made by Lindfors on Ekwensi was his view that Ekwensi 'has a knack for transplanting un-African events on to African soil', and that 'his is a literature of imitation and adaptation, not a literature of imagination and original invention'. Mr Lindfors' problem is understandable but unfortunate. He has a concept of the definition of African literature in which it is perfectly easy to rule out Ekwensi's writings without much ado. Ekwensi writes about the Africa of today, under the influence of today's economic pressures, politics, and conflict of values. The characters which emerge fail to appeal to the non-African critic as 'African' in his cultivated image from the days of Edgar Rice Burroughs' *Tarzan of the Apes* and Edgar Wallace's *Sanders of the River*. Perhaps as soon as Ekwensi writes a novel about black magic, ritual, medicine men, mud and thatched huts, banana leaves, palm trees, and rolling rivers, Mr Lindfors will cease to see his work as 'un-African and unimaginative'. I dare say he may have to wait too long.

Mr Lindfors thought that at the early part of his writing career, Ekwensi wrote children's and teenage books and only later on did he 'begin to reach an older audience'. On the contrary *People of the City* and *Iska*, both adult books, owe their origins to the same influences and experiences in Ekwensi's career that produced *When Love Whispers* and *Drummer Boy*, both teenage books. The raw materials for *People of the City* had been collected as far back as 1947 even though Mr Ekwensi wrote up the entire story on a thirteen-day boat trip to England in 1953. The *Drummer Boy* published in 1960 had had its draft in Ekwensi's diary in the early forties. Any attempt, such as Mr Lindfors makes, at trying to assess Ekwensi's artistic growth from the chronological order of the publication of his works is bound to be highly misleading. The same is true of trying to find out what chief factor in his career has influenced his portrayal of a particular character in any of his books. This is not so easy with a man who in a relatively short span of forty-eight years has crowded into his life, the professional experiences of a teacher, a journalist, a forestry officer, a pharmacist, a broadcaster, a features producer, a film writer, a dramatist, a journalist, a national director of Information Services, Head of a national Broadcasting Corporation, and a diplomat. Ekwensi's creative art is not as simple and therefore as fallible as it is imagined. He belongs to the school of writers who believe in experimenting with everything in order to expose anything. The cities he writes about are representative of African cities undergoing the tremors of transition. Both the characters and the setting of his novels are truly African. There is always that Africanness (which Ekwensi styles the characteristic psychology in the African) in the background of the settings as well as in the mannerisms and mode of interactions of the characters.

Ekwensi believes that although 'politics' awakens similar trends of thought in all peoples, its approach by an African is not necessarily the same as that of the American or Irish. The writer must discover this element of psychology which is inherent in the behaviour of the African and bring this out when he writes. This psychological characteristic is always present in the African in whatever creative situation he is placed whether in a historical, political or romantic novel. When a writer succeeds in portraying this authentic picture of the African and his setting, if none other, at least Africans themselves will recognise it. The setting produces Ekwensi's characters, just as the dominant element **7** in the characteristics of each character dictates his manner of speech and scale of values.

In spite of what Lindfors thinks is Ekwensi's motive for writing *Jagua Nana*, it must be said that the theme of this novel is in keeping with Ekwensi's stated involvement with African cities undergoing tremors of transition. The city is a terribly corrupting influence, a den for Ali Baba where the forty thieves have stored all their gold, and anyone who has the magic words can go and help himself. And sometimes greed traps the sesame and the thieves come back and stab the intruder to death as they did to Ali Baba's brother. This whole African struggle is a struggle to Africanise the city so that the good things of Western culture can be brought under control. The bitter pill in *Jagua Nana* is corruption in politics masked by the veneer of glamorous sex. Jagua is sophisticated but illiterate in English. Her reactions are primal. She has no inhibitions and does not distinguish between emotions. She likes you and you know it right away. She is simply raw and earthy and in every way un-diplomatic. But she is a real product of all the combinations of the tremors of the African city undergoing transition. There are Jaguas as well as Ashokas in this city but this does not mean – as Lindfors thinks – that they should all 'lose their virginities the same way'. Oladele Taiwo has aptly remarked that:

> His (Ekwensi's) language is always graphic and vivid; it can also be poetic. For example in *Burning Grass* we get a strong feeling of the rhythms of savannah life and the movement of cattle. [Lindfors discerns from these, the imprint of the western branding iron!] He is particularly good at describing the clothes people wear and indicating their significance. His choice of words, his creation of atmosphere are all very effective. It is details like these which build up the whole complex structure of city life which Ekwensi puts before us. Cyprian Ekwensi's realism is deliberate. His aim is not to make city life look more romantic or attractive than it is, but to present it as he knows and sees it. It is no secret that his attitude has offended many in high places. Man at times lives in ignorance of himself and does not always like to be told his failings. Ekwensi deserves our applause for having the courage to open the eyes of the city dwellers to the evils which they are perpetrating and to bring to their notice the possible undesirable effects of a social life which is morally lax and decadent.[7]

Doesn't this make one wonder if it is the same Ekwensi who to Lindfors 'lacks artistic discretion' and whose novels 'are still failures'.

Yet Bernth Lindfors is only a representative of a type of Western critic. The frightening idea is that this type is rapidly gaining ground. **8** Their approach is nearly always the same. Usually they raise a loud hue and cry surrounded on all fronts by a huge smoke screen. Then they blow up through the smoke, a violent outrage on an author in that form which Shakespeare characterised as possessing 'sound and fury' but 'signifying nothing'. But the sound itself is enough, for when it has been heard, the protagonist becomes the authority on the author he has so lambasted. Notice that in 1965 Dr Austin Shelton, in an article entitled 'The African Writer' (published in *The Muse* – University of Nigeria, Nsukka, Vol. 2, No. 2, March 1965), declared:

So much of the output of literature in English, and French too indeed by Africans is defensive and at times even filled with absurd protest.

Then he took up Chinua Achebe:
'A certain Nigerian novelist (whose name I dare not mention, lest I be blasted by him) at the end of one of his good novels tagged on a cheap melodramatic amateurish [notice the use of this term on Ekwensi by Lindfors] bit of propaganda about an English Commissioner ordering his messengers to cut down Okonkwo's body, and then thinking about the book he is going to write. The title of the cold-blooded Commissioner's book, of course, is *The Pacification of the Primitive Tribes of the Lower Niger* . . .

'The unnamed author could not be satisfied with writing a good story: he had to "prove" that he was African and that Englishmen were the good guys who made things fall apart . . .

'Perhaps it is a shame that so many things fell apart, but the people of Okonkwo's clan certainly did little to fight the "falling apart" of the "things", and, moreover unless there had been a pacification of the tribes of the lower Niger, this particular author would not be writing a novel, and would not be able to live as well as he does today.' This last bit compares well with the views of the British critic who called Achebe names for daring to suggest that things had fallen apart under the Western impact when Achebe was brought up by missionaries, educated up to university level on scholarship and is now enjoying a regular white man's post (in J. P. Clark's 'Our Literary Critics', *Nigeria Magazine*, No. 74, September 1962). One would tend to ask: 'So what?' Nevertheless, Dr Austin Shelton did make his point. He has since then been an authority not only on African literature but on Achebe's art. It would appear that Bernth Lindfors is on his way to being the authority on Ekwensi's art.

What many Western critics issue on African literature is a reflection of a profound lack of knowledge about African cultural traditions coupled with an ignorance of the existence, nature and depth of the **9** heritage of African oral literature. In most cases some vague literary background or a landing on an African soil has not been enough to correct this intellectual imbalance.

In spite of some of the consequently unsound views expressed by such critics, African literature has its roots in Africa and is neither an appendage to French or British literature nor yet an African replica of popular Western authors. It should be looked at objectively or not at all.

All this is not to say that African critics are setting themselves up to be the judges here qualified to assess the works of African authors. But perhaps they may be more disposed to offer their views on an African work in order solely to help the reader towards gaining a proper perspective of the author and the realities of his work. The situation as it now exists seems to be that a Peace Corps sojourn, a spell of field work in Africa, a conference on African literature, a graduate studentship in African literature in a Western university, any of these is enough to qualify one as an authority on African literature.

The inescapable consequence of this approach is a literary criticism which has not much to recommend it but either a feeling of smug patronage or outrage towards the African writers – what J. P. Clark has described as 'the jaundice of prejudice and injured pride ... which, because it is a disease comes on the critics without their knowing it'.[8]

Judging from what comes often from the pens of some of these critics, one cannot help but agree with Clark that 'between great learning and great ignorance, the gap is indeed thin'. It may sound like saying that African writers are very sensitive about outside criticism, but it may be best to close here with Chinua Achebe's reply that:

> We are not opposed to criticism but we are getting a little weary of all the special types of criticism which have been designed for us by people whose knowledge of us is very limited.[9]

NOTES

1. Edris Makward, 'African Approach to African Literature', a paper delivered to the African Studies Association in Los Angeles, 1968.
2. J. P. Clark, 'Our Literary Critics', *Nigeria Magazine*, No. 74, September 1962.
3. Elizabeth Pryse: 'Getting into Perspective', *Nigeria Magazine*, No. 74, September 1962.
4. Anne Tibble: *African English Literature*, Peter Owen, London. p. 100.

5. Wonodi Okogbule: 'The Role of Folk Tales in African Society', *Africa Report*, December 1965.
6. Arthur Ravenscroft: *Chinua Achebe*, Longmans, London, 1969, p. 8. See also: Miss A. G. Stock: 'Yeats and Achebe', *The Journal of Commonwealth Literature*, No. 5, 1968.
7. Oladele Taiwo: *An Introduction to West African Literature*, Nelson, 1967, p. 162.
8. J. P. Clark: 'Our Literary Critics', *op. cit.*
9. Chinua Achebe: 'Where Angels Fear to Tread', *Nigeria Magazine*, No. 75, December 1962.

The writer is grateful to Mr Cyprian Ekwensi for the series of interviews and discussions as well as other vital data granted him in November and December 1969, without which this paper would have been impossible to write.

Equiano's Round Unvarnished Tale

Paul Edwards

A contemporary review of Equiano's *Interesting Narrative*[1] speaks of it as a 'round unvarnished tale' ... with much truth and simplicity[2] and indeed it is this very quality which is likely to convince the reader of the book's authenticity. Equiano's friend, Ottobah Cugoano, a Fante who worked as manservant to the court painter Cosway in London, had published in 1787 his book 'Thoughts and Sentiments on the Evil of Slavery'; this was so rhetorical in style that many readers have expressed doubts about whether it could have been written by Cugoano at all. A comparison of the surviving manuscript letters of Cugoano with the text of his book[3] leaves no doubt that it must have been extensively revised and in many places entirely rewritten – there is some evidence pointing to Equiano himself as reviser.[4] In the case of Equiano's *Narrative*, the one existing manuscript letter indicates that Equiano would have been perfectly capable of writing his book, which is less elaborate than Cugoano's both in style and argument.[5] But a question I want to raise here is whether Equiano's style is quite as simple and 'unvarnished' as it might at first appear.

Equiano made no claim to be a literary artist, only a man telling the story of his life; and so it would be unreasonable to make close comparisons between his book and the works of the major writers of fiction and biography at that time. All the same, the situation of Equiano has a touch of both Robinson Crusoe and Gulliver: from one point of view, his is a story of economic and moral survival on the bleak rock of slavery, a study in initiative and adaptability not entirely unlike Robinson Crusoe's; and from another, it is a tale, like Gulliver's, of new perspectives gained by physical alienation, in this case of the black man in a white world. An important difference, of course, is that Crusoe, Gulliver, and their adventures, emerge largely from their creators' imaginations and have the distinctive marks of conscious creative artistry about them, whereas Equiano is apparently doing no more than trying to tell the direct truth about his own experience. At the same time, he has many of the qualities of the more interesting eighteenth century literary heroes, particularly those of Defoe, revealing himself in the narrative in a wholly convincing way and never resorting to affectation or self-display merely in an effort to sentimentalise and to conceal his true nature. At times he presents himself as entirely ignorant, confused and vulnerable, at others as boastful or self-seeking, and is always prepared to mock his own weaknesses, as in the comic account of the dying passenger from whom he and Captain Farmer are hoping to extract at least a small fortune:

> While we were here an odd circumstance happened to the captain and me, which disappointed us both a good deal. A silversmith, whom we had brought to this place some voyages before, agreed with the captain to return with us to the West Indies and promised at the same time to give the captain a great deal of money, having pretended to take a liking to him, and being, as we thought, very rich. But while we stayed to load our vessel this man was taken ill in a house where he worked, and in a week's time became very bad. The worse he grew the more he used to speak of giving the captain what he had promised him, so that he expected something considerable from the death of this man, who had no wife or child, and he attended him day and night. I used also to go with the captain at his own desire, to attend him, especially when we saw there was no appearance of his recovery: and in order to recompence me for my trouble, the Captain promised me ten pounds when he should get the man's property. I thought this would be of great service to me, although I had nearly money enough to purchase my freedom if I should get safe this voyage to Montserrat. In this expectation I laid out above eight pounds of my money for a suit of superfine clothes to dance with at my freedom which I hoped was then at hand. We still continued to attend this man and were with him even on the last day he lived till very late at night, when we went on board. After we were got to bed, about one or two o'clock in the morning, the captain

was sent for and informed the man was dead. On this he came to my bed, and waking me, informed me of it, and desired me to get up and procure a light, and immediately go to him. I told him I was very sleepy and wished he would take somebody else with him; or else, as the man was dead and could want no further attendance, to let all things remain as they were till the next morning. 'No, no', said he, 'we will have the money tonight, I cannot wait till tomorrow, so let us go.' Accordingly I got up and struck a light, and away we both went and saw the man as dead as we could wish. The captain said he would give him a grand burial in gratitude for the promised treasure, and desired that all the things belonging to the deceased might be brought forth. Amongst others, there was a nest of trunks of which he had kept the keys whilst the man was ill, and when they were produced we opened them with no small eagerness and expectation; and as there were a great number within one another, with much impatience we took them one out of the other. At last, when we came to the smallest and opened it, we saw it was full of papers, which we supposed to be notes, at the sight of which our heart leapt for joy, and that instant the captain, clapping his hands, cried out, 'Thank God, here it is.' But when we took up the trunk and began to examine the supposed treasure and long-looked-for bounty, (alas! alas! how uncertain and deceitful are all human affairs!) what had we found! While we thought we were embracing a substance we grasped an empty nothing. The whole amount that was in the nest of trunks was only one dollar and a half, and all that the man possessed would not pay for his coffin. Our sudden and exquisite joy was now succeeded by as sudden and exquisite pain, and my captain and I exhibited for some time most ridiculous figures – pictures of chagrin and disappointment! We went away greatly mortified and left the deceased to do as well as he could for himself as we had taken so good care of him when alive for nothing. (pp. 93–5)

At another point in the *Narrative* he confesses to putting a lighted candle into a barrel of gunpowder:

Just as our ship was under sail, I went down into the cabin to do some business, and had a lighted candle in my hand, which, in my hurry, without thinking, I held in a barrel of gunpowder. It remained in the powder until it was near catching fire, when fortunately I observed it and snatched it out in time, and providentially no harm happened; but I was so overcome with terror that I immediately fainted at this deliverance. (p. 130)

Yet within a few pages our hero is at it again! This time he has carried his candle into Dr Irving's store room:

This little place was stuffed with all manner of combustibles, particularly with tow and aquafortis, and many other dangerous things. Unfortunately it happened in the evening as I was writing my journal that I had occasion to take the candle out of the lantern, and a spark having touched a single thread of the tow, all the rest caught flame, and immediately the whole was in a blaze. I saw nothing but present death before me and expected to be the first to perish in the flames. In a moment the alarm was spread and many people who were near ran to assist in putting out the fire. All the time I was in the very midst of the flames. My shirt and the handkerchief on my neck were burnt and I was almost smothered with the smoke. However, through God's mercy, as I was nearly giving up all hopes, some people brought blankets and mattresses and threw them on the flames, by which means in a short time the fire was put out. I was severely reprimanded and menaced by such of the officers who knew it, and strictly charged never more to go there with a light: and, indeed, even my own fears made me give heed to this command for a little time, but at last, not being able to write my journal in any other part of the ship, I was tempted again to venture by stealth with a light into the same cabin, though not without considerable fear and dread on my mind. (pp. 132–3)

So, while the author deliberately reveals himself in these instances in a comical or grotesque light, this is balanced by our recognition that self-mockery implies self-knowledge; tensions are set up in our response to the narrator, so that even his devotion to writing his journal gives to the comic a touch of the heroic. Self-revelation through self-mockery is a persistent feature of the *Narrative* – see for instance the episode of the grampuses (pp. 37–8) or the wild ride on horseback (pp. 54–5). The comic possibilities are never avoided in an effort to adopt heroic or pathetic postures, and in consequence the author's character as narrator of his own tale is seen in deeper perspective.

Still more interesting are the ambivalent feelings which Equiano displays from time to time for those who help him, particularly in chapters nine and ten, where there is considerable tension between the affection he feels for Captain Farmer, and the nagging irritation of his subordinate place in life: what becomes apparent is Equiano's need to release himself not only from his enemies, but also from his friends. This whole section offers a remarkable example of the psychology of subordination, as regret for Farmer's death mingles inextricably with the pleasure Equiano feels (and is prepared to reveal as having its boastful and complacent side) about the opportunity which Farmer's death has given him to display his own skills as a navigator and leader of men:

The whole care of the vessel rested therefore upon me, and I was obliged to direct her by mere dint of reason, not being able to work a traverse. The captain was now very sorry he had not taught me navigation, and protested, if ever he should get well again, he would not fail to do so; but in about seventeen days his illness increased so **15**

much, that he was obliged to keep his bed, continuing sensible, however, till the last, constantly having the owner's interest at heart; for
this just and benevolent man ever appeared much concerned about
the welfare of what he was intrusted with. When this dear friend
found the symptoms of death approaching, he called me by my
name; and, when I came to him, he asked (with almost his last
breath,) if he had ever done me any harm? 'God forbid I should think
so,' replied I, 'I should then be the most ungrateful of wretches to the
best of benefactors'. While I was thus expressing my affection and
sorrow by his bed, he expired without saying another word; and the
day following we committed his body to the deep. Every man on
board loved him and regretted his death; but I was exceedingly
affected at it, and found that I did not know, till he was gone, the
strength of my regard for him. Indeed, I had every reason in the
world to be attached to him; for, besides that he was in general mild,
affable, generous, faithful, benevolent, and just, he was to me a friend
and father; and had it pleased Providence, that he had died about five
months before, I verily believe I should not have obtained my freedom when I did; and it is not improbable that I might not have been
able to get it at any rate afterwards.

The captain being dead, the mate came on the deck, and made such
observations as he was able, but to no purpose. In the course of a few
days more, the few bullocks that remained were found dead; but the
turkies I had, though on deck, and exposed to so much wet and bad
weather, did well, and I afterwards gained near three hundred per
cent. on the sale of them; so that in the event it proved a happy
circumstance for me that I had not brought the bullocks I intended,
for they must have perished with the rest; and I could not help looking on this, otherwise trifling circumstance, as a particular providence of God, and was thankful accordingly. The care of the vessel
took up all my time, and engaged my attention entirely. As we were
now out of the variable winds, I thought I should not be much puzzled to hit upon the islands. I was persuaded I steered right for Anti-
gua, which I wished to reach, as the nearest to us; and in the course of
nine or ten days we made the island, to our great joy, and the day
after, we came safe to Montserrat.

Many were surprised when they heard of my conducting the sloop
into the port, and I now obtained a new appellation, and was called
Captain. This elated me not a little, and it was quite flattering to my
vanity to be thus styled by as high a title as any freeman in this place
possessed. When the death of the captain became known, he was
much regretted by all who knew him; for he was a man universally
respected. At the same time the sable captain lost no fame; for the
success I had met with, increased the affection of my friends in no
small measure. (pp. 102–4)

There are a number of reversal situations like this in the narrative. For
instance, the former slave who has been saved by the paternalistic at-
tentions of others, dreams that his master's ship was 'wrecked amidst

the surfs and rocks, and that I was the means of saving every one on board' (p. 105). The dream comes true. As in the previous chapter, Equiano again takes over from the ship's captain, and remarks with some satisfaction on the superior conduct of the 'three black men and a Dutch creole sailor' to that of the white men (p. 109). Significantly, when the Captain orders the hatches to be nailed down on the slaves in the hold, Equiano the former slave takes over from him and the hatches are not nailed down (p. 108). Of course, this is not to say that the racial attitudes taken up by Equiano are simple ones for the white men of his experience form a very mixed company, and for this reason his responses to the world into which he has been thrown at the age of eleven are bound to be complex, as the episode of the death of Captain Farmer shows. But the emancipation of the slave Equiano is brought about by more than the mere payment of forty pounds sterling: he also has to act out roles of dominance through which he can shed his past.

It might be unwise to make much of the rhetorical passages in the *Narrative* in view of the doubts that have been expressed about whether these might not have been added by another hand, but there is really no good reason why Equiano, an avid reader of eighteenth-century religious tracts as well as the Bible and (bearing in mind his frequent quotations) at least the first two books of *Paradise Lost*, should not have written with some degree of expansive eloquence. But these passages are in a way less interesting than the plainer ones. One reason for thinking them to be additions by another author might be their occurrence alongside episodes described in a very much plainer language, and nowhere is this more marked than in Chapter 2, which begins in the plain style and ends with a fine rhetorical flourish. But if we look closely at this chapter it becomes clear that these two manners of writing are being used deliberately and appropriately, and that the plain style is in a sense the subtler of the two. This style occurs in its most naïve form when Equiano is describing his initial fear and perplexity at the ways of the white men:

> One white man in particular I saw, when we were permitted to be on deck, flogged so unmercifully with a large rope near the foremast, that he died in consequence of it; and they tossed him over the side as they would have done a brute. This made me fear these people the more; and I expected nothing less than to be treated in the same manner. I could not help expressing my fears and apprehensions to some of my countrymen; I asked them if these people had no country, but lived in this hollow place? (the ship): they told me they did not, but came from a distant one. 'Then,' said I, 'how comes it in all our country we never heard of them?' They told me because they lived so very far off. I then asked where were their women? had they

17

any like themselves? I was told they had. 'And why,' said I, 'do we not see them?' They answered, because they were left behind. I asked how the vessel could go? they told me they could not tell; but that there was cloth put upon the masts by the help of the ropes I saw, and then the vessel went on; and the white men had some spell or magic they put in the water when they liked, in order to stop the vessel. I was exceedingly amazed at this account, and really thought they were spirits. I therefore wished much to be from amongst them for I expected they would sacrifice me; but my wishes were vain – for we were so quartered that it was impossible for any of us to make our escape. (pp. 27–8)

What is distinctive here is Equiano's skill in creating a dramatic language, not merely to describe in literal terms, but to recreate the very sense of the speakers' childhood simplicity and incomprehension and to distinguish this from an articulate and informed 'present'. Thus objects are described in naïve terms – the ship is 'this hollow place', the sails 'cloth put upon the mast' and the anchor becomes 'some spell or magic they put upon the water, when they liked, to stop the vessel.' Equiano does not merely write about his perplexity; his language becomes, dramatically, that of the perplexed boy he once was. This is true of the whole dialogue, in the naïve assumption behind 'how comes it in all our country we never heard of them?', the implied ignorance of the more 'knowledgeable' people who are replying to the boy's questions, and the very simplicity of the sentences in which question and response are formed, itself suggesting an innocent, untutored view of life.

Many of the best effects of the *Narrative*, in fact, are gained by this kind of dramatic or ironic simplicity – the episode of the dying man on board the ship already referred to (pp. 93–5), the account of Equiano's petty trading and the theft of the bags of fruit (pp. 79–80) or of yet another reversal situation, where the Indians are the perplexed innocents and Equiano is now in the position of authority and wisdom. Notice in particular how a complex sentence structure and a literary vocabulary are suddenly and dramatically discarded for particular effect. Equiano is describing the conduct of the drunken Indian Governor who,

getting quite drunk, grew very unruly and struck one of our most friendly chiefs, who was our nearest neighbour, and also took his gold-laced hat from him. At this a great commotion took place, and the Doctor interfered to make peace as we could all understand one another, but to no purpose; and at last they became so outrageous that the Doctor, fearing he might get into trouble, left the house and made the best of his way to the nearest wood, leaving me to do as well as I could among them. I was so enraged with the Governor that

I could have wished to have seen him tied fast to a tree and flogged for his behaviour, but I had not people enough to cope with his party. I therefore thought of a stratagem to appease the riot. Recollecting a passage I had read in the life of Columbus when he was amongst the Indians in Mexico or Peru, where on some occasion he frightened them by telling them of certain events in the heavens, I had recourse to the same expedient, and it succeeded beyond my most sanguine expectations. When I had formed my determination I went in the midst of them, and, taking hold of the Governor, I pointed up to the heavens. I menaced him and the rest: I told them God lived there, and that he was angry with them, and they must not quarrel so; that they were all brothers, and if they did not leave off and go away quietly, I would take the book (pointing to the Bible), read, and *tell* God to make them dead. This was something like magic. The clamour immediately ceased and I gave them some rum and a few other things, after which they went away peaceably, and the Governor afterwards gave our neighbour, who was called Captain Plasmyah, his hat again. When the Doctor returned he was exceedingly glad at my success in thus getting rid of our troublesome guests. (pp. 145-6)

It is worth noting that up to this point, the Indians have been established as at least moderately noble savages, with many of the virtues of Equiano's 'Eboes' of the opening chapters, and capable of being compared advantageously to the Europeans. But it is at this moment that the drunken Indian Governor appears to disrupt the happy proceedings, the situation being saved by the trickery of the original white adventurer Columbus, the doctrines of European Christianity, and the sharp wit of an African ex-slave, who adds, characteristically, a note on Dr Irving's reliance on him to settle the situation. The effects gained by Equiano in his narrative are often, it seems to me, conscious artistic effects; they may at times be unconscious; but one thing must be clear, that his simplicities are really not quite so simple.

NOTES

1. *The Interesting Narrative of the Life of Olaudah Equiano, or Gustavus Vassa the African*, London 1789. All quotations in this article are from *Equiano's Travels*, ed. Paul Edwards, Heinemann Educational Books 1967. The full text of the *Narrative* will shortly be avilable in a facsimile reprint of the 1st edition, published by Dawsons of Pall Mall in their Colonial History Series. The present writer has contributed a detailed introduction and notes to this reprint, and this article is a slightly extended version of the last part of the introduction.
2. *The General Magazine and Impartial Review*, July 1789.
3. These letters are printed in an appendix to *Thoughts and Sentiments*, **19**

etc. ed. Paul Edwards, Dawsons of Pall Mall 1969, and are discussed in the introduction to the same volume.

4. There are striking similarities between a report sent by Equiano from Plymouth, quoted in the *Public Advertiser*, 4 April 1787, and a passage in Cugoano's *Thoughts and Sentiments.*

5. For the text of this letter and a discussion of its implications, see *Notes and Queries*, June 1968, pp. 222–5. The text of the letter will also be printed in the reprint of the *Narrative* to be published by Dawsons, and the 2nd edition of *Equiano's Travels.*

The Novels of Onuora Nzekwu

G. D. Killam

Onuora Nzekwu is among the first wave of Nigerian novelists. He has published three novels – *Wand of Noble Wood* (1961), *Blade Among the Boys* (1962) and *Highlife for Lizards* (1965) – which reflect the same concerns as the fiction of say, Chinua Achebe and Cyprian Ekwensi. Yet the amount of criticism devoted to Nzekwu is small, confined for the most part to reviews of the three books, and to brief statements in the critical commentaries of Judith Gleason, Robert July (in the Beier *Black Orpheus* critical anthology), Taiwo's *Introduction To African Literature*, and more recently Margaret Laurence's *Long Drums and Cannons*. At the moment, therefore, what matters is that the critical issues posed by his work should be raised so as to suggest his place among his peers.

This essay is really an introduction which attempts to present a few critical notes that will isolate the problems faced by Nzekwu's readers, to make a number of general statements about his work and then to discuss specifically the three novels, in the belief that Nzekwu is important enough a writer to merit attention and consideration.

In saying that Nzekwu's subject matter is typical of the first wave of **21** novels out of Black Africa we mean that Nzekwu explores the various ways in which Africa and Africans have been influenced by the presence of Europe and European values: his novels reveal the difficulty of adjustment between two civilisations and the ways in which he tries to accommodate himself to the changes which have taken place as a result of the forces – political, economic, religious – of western culture. His novels offer, therefore, through the various situations they present, attempts at an imaginative assessment of the gains and losses derived by Africans from contact with Europe. His work is charged by some with being too 'anthropological' (of this more later) and with being directed too explicitly at foreign readers. It is important to note with others, that his principal concern is with matters of relevance to his own country and society and not with interpreting European values *per se*.

Technically there is nothing experimental in his novels of the kind one finds in Okara, Soyinka, or, more recently, Kwei Armah. For him the novel is a fixed form, the vehicle for narrative exposition, fairly carefully designed even if loose and episodic. For the most part he composes the kind of novel in which the plot stands out and in which characters are portrayed through their actions rather than through an exploration of their psychology. (It is important to note that this is not to insist that some of the events that the novels display are apprehended in rational terms, but merely that even the magical element in the first two books out of which their major imaginative achievement arises is given to us in literal fashion. More must and will be made of this feature of the writing.)

Nzekwu, further, is a writer of more limited scope than his peers. The historic span of the novels ranges between the 1910s and the early 1960s. That is, he does not press as far backward in time as Achebe in *Things Fall Apart* nor as far forward as Achebe in *A Man Of The People* or Kwei Armah in *The Beautyful Ones Are Not Yet Born*. He confines himself to those events and circumstances which shaped in a general way the broad cultural patterns of Nigerian life under the impact of Europe. The general social range is also narrow, dealing usually with the dilemmas of Nigerians who attempt to achieve a balance between western civilisation and traditional culture, and with personal relationships as these have been defined by the new conventions which have emerged.

Nzekwu's style can be terse and exact, which is in the tradition of realistic writing, and is capable of evoking a sense of place and event which gives the reader all he needs to know of the scenes and actions before him. Yet too often the narrative is marred by solid interpolations of anthropological and sociological data. It is for the most part a prose of explication rather than implication. In the third novel, *Highlife For Lizards*, he dramatises materials which he merely expounds in the earlier two novels and the result is more compelling and convincing than with the earlier books.

Within these limits, Nzekwu is a serious writer. He is concerned with issues of social, cultural, political and religious consequence at the individual and the societal levels. His novels display their concerns and conclusions through stories of personal relationships which reflect problems of belief, choice, and action, central to a generality of contemporary Nigerians. If there is none of the variety of devices which characterise, say, Achebe's or Soyinka's work – the irony, the fierce and abrasive satire, the gift for caricature, the cold assault on the failures of individuals and society – neither are there any false consolations offered. Nzekwu is a less finished artist than some of his peers; yet he is serious in exploiting the social role of the writer. Perhaps it is fair to say that Nzekwu is essentially a novelist of manners, by which we mean that he is concerned almost exclusively with the variety of problems which confront his own generation, the group of people in transition between the traditional and the modern, who are in an important sense unique since they sum up the ambiguities created by the impact of colonialism on traditional culture and make discoveries about their own natures, values and beliefs, which preclude the generation which follows them from being like them. It is not so much a difference from other cultures that distinguishes the men and women who appear in Nzekwu's novels – since the histories of all peoples comprise a continuous process of growth and modification – but rather a matter of the intensity of this difference.

Wand of Noble Wood is Nzekwu's first attempt at revealing the dilemma which confronts the modern Nigerian who tries to strike a balance between traditional and western culture. The hero of the novel, Peter Obiesie, is a westernised Ibo man who works as a reporter in Lagos. (In some respects he resembles Amuso Sango, the hero of Ekwensi's *People of the City*, though it is important to note that Peter's career as a journalist does not involve him in the pressing social and political life of the country as it is consolidated in the capital city, nor is the city itself the subject of Nzekwu's book as it is in Ekwensi's.) The ostensible subject of the book is marriage, and subordinate themes are related to this. Peter Obiesie has reached the age of thirty without marrying, and his friends and family are becoming concerned. Chapter 4 and 6 of the novel explain why Peter has failed to marry; it is partly a matter of his achieving the bride price, partly a matter of observing the custom which enjoins him to wait until his two senior brothers have married. A **23** larger issue is, however, at stake as the following passage suggests, a passage which specifies the particular subject of *Wand of Noble Wood*; a subject to which all the other comment of the novel relates. Peter says to his friends Reg and Nora ('. . . a West Indian girl [whom] the author evidently introduced . . . because it gives him a chance to explain some important Ibo customs to her and, incidentally, to his foreign readers'):[1]

> It is the problem of overcoming the dilemma created by the conflict between tradition and westernism, a problem arising out of our attempt to blend present relative practices with worthy concepts which tradition has established. That, in short, is the crux of the matter. (p. 47)[2]

So that while Peter is a modern man who admits that many customs are out of date, he nevertheless supports the idea of the continuity and worth of Ibo family social ties that such customs suggest. When Peter's two brothers decide to marry he decides to return to his village, Ado, to seek a bride. According to custom the bride must also be an Ibo girl. She must come from the same family group, but must not be related more closely than the fourth generation. If any disease can be traced in her lineage she will be unacceptable. These obstacles are formidable enough but Peter overcomes them in finding Nneka, a schoolmistress (and thus like himself a modern person) who fulfils, it seems, all the qualifications required – no relationship between the families can be traced, no disease is apparent, her father is a highly respected member of the community. Negotiations between the two families begin when suddenly (and somewhat improbably in terms of the logic of the plot) the father reveals that the curse of *Iyi-ocha* has been laid on Nneka's mother and so, because it has not been removed, she still bears it. However, Peter and Nneka (with the assistance of a wise uncle) perform certain rites, the curse is absolved and they are free to marry. But Nneka dies by her own hand on the night before the wedding – it turns out the curse has not been successfully absolved due to the interference of a jealous and evil suitor who removed 'the white stone, the most important item in the *Iyi-ocha*'. Given this, were Nneka to marry Peter, he would die. Such is the quality and strength of Nneka's love that she prefers Peter's life to her own. After her death Peter becomes the symbol of the distracted lover – 'there was no doubt that I had suffered much in that period and that I was still suffering. It was evident from my worn-out appearance. I was thin and emaciated. I was a skeleton of myself. Depression and sadness had replaced life and the joy to live which characterised me. My clothes hung on me as if from a peg. I was no longer mentally alert.' (p. 139).

(A kind of happy ending is eventually achieved as Peter is reconciled with a former mistress who had borne him a child.)

So much for plot. The novel tells the personal tragedy of Peter and Nneka. But it attempts to do more. It seems to establish the various obstacles that confront them and the tragedy which overtakes them as a metaphor of the wider cultural class between traditional and modern values and beliefs, between past and present.

The importance of the novel in terms of the symbolic statement it makes lies in the fact that the proposal of marriage between Peter and Nneka, because of who they are and where they are – westernised Ibos aware of the possibilities which western values offer them yet devoted to certain important values of their own culture – and the fate which overtakes them, mirrors the wider attempt at marriage between the two cultures, traditional and modern. Their personal tragedy reflects the inability of society 'to effect a conciliation between the past and the present, to find the right balance between inherited culture and acquired European values.'[3] But this does not imply the triumph of conservatism since the curse was not absolved not because their peers wished to destroy them or their love, but because a jealous suitor wanted to subvert legitimate conduct to his own evil purposes.

Nevertheless, Peter and Nneka are victims of their place in time when belief of a religious kind supported by mystical/magical elements is powerfully believed in; the rational assessments of Nneka and Peter count for nothing against the force of the *Iyi-ocha*.

The confrontation between traditional and modern values, vested principally in the events which shape the affairs of Peter and Nneka, is elaborated in various comparisons between African culture and Western practices throughout the novel, and these relate to concerns which are political, religious, economic and other. The following series of quotations reveals the variety of comment of this kind which the novel offers.

The passage, already cited above, becomes a statement of the generalised concern of the novel.

It is the problem of overcoming the dilemma created by the conflict between tradition and westernism, the problem arising out of our attempt to blend present relative social practices with worthy concepts which tradition has established. That, in short, is the crux of the matter. (p. 47)

And this is further elaborated by such comments as follow:

Because, while absorbing the best in foreign cultures, we must also **25** retain what is best in our own. Only the best is good enough for the African. (p. 30)

And further by this:

> In many advanced countries their bonds have been completely broken, yet they have not fully emerged from the state of mind resulting from that subjection. (p. 30)

And by this:

> Fortunately, Nora said hopefully, 'This traditional social set-up is breaking down and will soon be completely gone. Africans are becoming more individualistic nowadays.' (p. 27)

These in turn are elaborated by a long discussion on pages 52 to 54 about Christianity in the African context which concludes with the following passage, which specifies the relative lack of strength of the appeal Christianity can make to the African:

> Go among the grownups who profess Christianity. The moment they can afford it they become polygamists and take Ozo and other traditional titles. When they think it will do them good they consult fortunetellers, make charms and wear them, and do a thousand and one other things which, to their tens of African priests, who themselves mimic their white brother clerics, are purely 'idolatrous and un-Christian.'

> Christianity is at heart; it is not the priest, the building, or the worship. Denominationalism is a deceit, and attendance at church is a matter of convenience. The fault with Christian missionaries is that they are blind to the good in our traditional religion. If they could only see them and introduce them into their system, Christianity would be less foreign to us. Look at the Cherubin and Seraphim Society. Why, do you think, does it appeal to many of our people.

Further, explicit comment is offered about the influence of the Western on the African culture and is found in a discussion of the implications to African society by the introduction of European monetary methods into traditional practices, another factor which contributes to the breaking down of traditional values. The discussion centres on the question of the bride price, but its general application is apparent:

> Cash economy has replaced the agricultural economy of our ancestors ... When cash economy developed, suitors switched over to using money in place of farm produce. Again each suitor tried to

outdo the other. It came to the stage where it became a racket. Parents dictated a bride price for their girls and suitors tried to beat it down. But the girl always went to the highest bidder. Marriage as an essence has disappeared and love with it ... The average girl assumes that she will marry a man who can support her. The assumption is based on the fact that it is men who create wealth and have the governance of property ... But ... it does not conform with our traditional way of life. The ideal thing is for a woman to contribute toward the family fortune. That is how our society understands it ...

Nzekwu here introduces an argument similar to that dramatised by Achebe in *Things Fall Apart* and the sequence of novels which follow it, that colonialism allowed the materialistic principle to become dominant over the spiritual, which in turn was undermined by Christianity. The traditional balance was thus upset, and materialism became the dominant pursuit of the people. This is, of course, merely an element in Nzekwu's total argument and not, as in Achebe's work, central.

These literal comments on the factors which have brought about change in civil life as a result of the presence of a more powerful and foreign culture is humanised by those scenes devoted to displaying the force of the magical/mystical element in Ibo life. There is no paradox here for in the area where the magical element in traditional religious belief works to influence and direct the lives of the characters, we see not only that religion is subject to the same sorts of external pressures as those mentioned but that its inclusion elaborates those scenes, that it survives and dominates. We have already seen how the force of the *Iyi-ocha* works on Nneka and Peter to produce personal tragedy; and this has been prepared for in two important scenes earlier in the novel. And it is important to note that here Nzekwu is at his best as an imaginative artist, for in these scenes he is working not at the level of the objective and disinterested reporter of the customs of his people, but rather on the imaginative and emotional level of participant in these beliefs.

The first of these scenes is found in chapter 5 of the novel where Peter visits Mr Agbata, an elderly gentleman who is ill and close to death. Mr Agbata babbles about the power of his magic and how it has assisted him in taking vengeance on his enemies at various times – he confesses 'what wicked things he did and enumerates the names of all he killed – those who offended him and those he used as guinea pigs for newly acquired magic powers.' Mr Odinfe, the nurse, in attempting to account for the reasons Agbata cannot die says 'Perhaps he has one of these magic threads that chain life to a dying body,' and advises Peter and his friends to make a thorough search of the old man's house. Agbata himself provides an enigmatic clue by saying: 'You know that goat that **27** always refuses to leave the kitchen? It has no heart. If you can discover its heart, then you will know why you cannot kill me.' (He further enjoins Peter 'Do not neglect our traditions . . . They are so very rich.') A search of the house is fruitless and finally the old man tells Peter and his friend to remove a board at the side of the bed.

The space was empty, but at a point underneath his pillow, hanging from the spring of the bed, was a string of black, red, and yellow threads. At the other end of it was the fresh bleeding heart of a goat. Surprisingly the heart was contracting and expanding. It was suspended over a hole dug in the floor.

'Do you see the string there?' the dying man asked, and no one answered.

'That heart suspended from it,' he continued, 'is the heart of that goat in the kitchen . . . It will always be . . . to you a wonder . . . how it ever left the goat. . . . My powers are great . . . I can give them to you . . . but you are too young . . . And you will misuse them . . . That heart came to be there even before you were born.' He paused. 'I am tired. . . . I want to go home.' He paused again, breathing with more difficulty. 'Cut the thread,' he added, but no one moved.

'Cut the thread,' he said again, and one of the men who had followed us from the hospital went under the bed with a kitchen knife and cut it. As the heart fell into the hole, two things happened: the dying man breathed his last. The old goat bleated urgently, 'KPAA!' and became silent. A servant rushed in to report that the old goat had died for no apparent cause. Of course, we knew better how this man and his old goat had passed away.

Here we find writing of the kind which informs Achebe's short stories, especially, *The Sacrificial Egg* and *Akueke*. Nothing is explained, since religious beliefs of this kind are an anathema to rational scrutiny. Here is mystery and it remains mystery. The same is true of the *Iyi-ocha*. 'The curse is meant to work: because the white stone was stolen.' We are told how the curse operated, but not *why*. But the psychological consequences of the events are left behind and promote desolation, loss, and tragedy.

The second passage is found in chapter 16 where Peter is visited by the 'Ghost Voice' of his uncle Azoba, dead now for years. The passage is worth citing at length for in it the various themes of the novel are drawn together:

'I am indeed your guardian angel. I want you to follow the right way, the way of our fathers,' the voice answered with a laugh, 'Why do you wonder at things that happen under cover of darkness?

'Have you tried to understand why, nowadays, corruption and ill-will are the order of the day among our people?

'Do not close your eyes to facts.' The voice sounded aggrieved. 'Has not witchcraft spread and are witches not daily harming people and proving more destructive than they were in the past? Does brother not fear brother these days? Does one not regard the other as a wolf to him? Here is the community life established by our ancestors not broken up through fear? Do people not cheat and lie and steal because they want to be rich at the expense of others? Are these things not true?

'Do people live as long as our fathers did? Are our people as strong as our fathers were? Are they as hard-working? Are they as honest?

'Have we not openly despised our traditional heritage? How many of our people are proud of the exploits of their fathers? How many of them know their folklores and fables, their history and background their relatives and what their relationship is?

'Where is our vast wealth of cultural heritage? Where are our wall-paintings, where are our beautiful patterns, delicately painted on the bodies by our women? Have they not all become the bushman's concern? Where is our music? How many of our traditional pieces are still remembered? What is happening to our traditional architecture? Are they not fast deteriorating?

'What respect is left for our traditional religion? Are not ninety per cent of our people who profess they are Christians really half Christian and half pagan? Does your present foreign religion bind together all aspects of life so that we do not degenerate into a horrible and wicked people, people without a past? Does your new religion throw out in every fibre of present-day social, economic, and political life as did our traditional religion of old? Does it permeate every phase of your modern civilisation as traditional religion did to traditional culture?

'Not by neglect of our gods and failure to satisfy the many deceased ancestors who have been buried in this fashion. Their spirits are taking revenge on our people for our failure to adhere to the wisdom handed down to them through the generations. The gods are angry. Their ancestors are angry. Our people must come back to them. They must revive all those aspects of our cultural life which have been dropped or allowed to go to pieces. They must revive them just as they have revived the age-grade societies. They must retrace their steps if peace and harmony are to reign.' (pp. 115–16)

The passage reveals as well a principal fault in Nzekwu's writing which compromises his main achievement. Too often he overworks his material, succumbs to the temptation to explain and have his characters become *raissoneurs*. This feature of his writing was identified early by, among others, Omigidi Aragbabalu and the comment he makes should be sufficient to make the point. He chooses as his example the beginning of chapter 7 where Nzekwu writes:

Among us Kola nut is a highly valued and indispensable product. It commands our respect in a way no other produce has done. Though it **29** is one of the commonest vegetable products seen in Nigeria, it represents in our society a vital, social and religious element. Kola nut is a symbol of friendship, the proper offering at meetings and religious occasions. Its presentation to a guest surpasses any other sign of hospitality which any host among us can show, even though in some places it costs only a penny. (pp. 47–8)

And goes on to observe 'all this is really quite unnecessary because the author . . . makes us witness the prayer of Cousin Mbanefo when splitting the Kola nut, and this prayer in itself is completely enough to explain to the non-Nigerian reader what a Kola nut is. But the prayer is part of the plot – the previous explanatory passage was not':[4]

'Creator of the universe, view Kola nut. Our ancestoral spirits, through Kola nut. He who brings Kola nut brings life. Wherever a child may be, may it wake with each dawn. We will all live. Forward jumps the male monkey; it never jumps backwards. If a kite and an eagle perch, whichever says the other should not perch, may its wings break. Whatever one's occupation, may it provide for his old age.' (p. 48)

That is, in the latter passage Nzekwu transposes to the level of imaginative art the literal, matter-of-fact explication of the former. This happens too rarely in the novel. The novel works mostly at the literal level and that is why, in the end, it is unsatisfactory as a work of imagination, as a piece of literature. Because of his tendency to explain rather than to create life in the novel we as readers stand in the same relation to the novel as does Peter Obiesie – both we and he are spectators rather than participants in the events the novel displays.

Blade Among the Boys is much the same in form and subject as *Wand of Noble Wood*. The construction of the novel is, if anything, more episodic than the first book and Nzekwu takes the opportunity that such a structure affords to include much description and exposition of the nature of Ibo life and customs. The geographic range is greater in that the hero of the novel, Patrick Ikenga, is an Ibo, born in Kafanchan in Northern Nigeria where the first part of the book is set. This affords the author the opportunity of commenting on the customs of the various ethnic groups who comprise the population of the heterogeneous northern railway and commercial towns. But apart from one return visit to the north, to Zaria, most of the action takes place in various southern Nigerian towns – Lagos, Ado, Port Harcourt and Enugu.

As was the case with *Wand of Noble Wood*, *Blade Among the Boys* is a problem novel and deals with the difficulty of an individual in striking a balance between the attractions of a new and imported culture and the demands placed on him by his own traditions. The dilemma in which the hero finds himself is centred in religion. The expanded treatment which this subject receives in *Blade Among the Boys* is foreshadowed in a scene, incidental to the main action, in *Wand of Noble Wood*, part of which was cited above. Peter Obiesie's uncle Mbanefo is voicing his complaint against Christian missionary activities, and says:

> 'You must understand,' Mbanefo said, settling himself more comfortably in his seat, 'that I do not deny any of the things she says the missionaries have done for us. These things are all on the material plane. I am only critical of their methods, which condemn everything traditional. Look at it from the spiritual angle. Did they try to study our religious heritage so as to find out if it contained any good things? No. Without trying to understand it, they condemned our traditional way of life which saw our ancestors through the centuries. They called us savages and barbarians and tried to impose their own way of life on us. That was very wrong and made us suspicious of their intentions.
>
> 'But they buttressed their teachings with material services which they rendered us. Apart from hospitals and schools, they made us presents of clothes and sometimes food. Thus they won not our spirits but our bodies; not a true belief in their teaching but our presence at their services.' (p. 53)

Nzekwu consolidates his theme in the story of Patrick Ikenga and his responses to the many obstacles placed before him on his way to becoming a priest of the Roman Catholic church. A devout boy of religious parents, he conceives his ideal of becoming a priest while very young. When his father dies, Peter returns to his ancestral home in Ado in Iboland. He attends Mass for a time with the other members of his family, and worships his ancestors at the same time. As his manhood approaches, and despite the fact that he is the custodian of one of the highest traditional offices in the political/religious structure of his people – that of *Okpala*, the spiritual head of the family, both living and dead – he rejects ancestor worship in order to devote the whole of his life to the Christian faith. In Holy Trinity College in Lagos, he raises questions about policies in the school – 'As a priest, I ought to be able to defend my faith and justify the methods adopted for its spread; at least, among my own people' – which incurs the censure of the Fathers and Patrick is expelled from the school. For a time he works for the railways, a post got for him through an uncle who bribes an official of the company. Patrick himself participates in the complicated system of nepotism and bribery at work, it is suggested, in nearly all the areas of Nigerian life. But his spiritual desires reassert themselves and once more **31** he enters a seminary to fulfil his youthful ambition. His decision enrages his uncle, Ononye, the guardian of Patrick and a symbol of traditional culture, and destroys his mother who sees in his decision a denial of his birthright and the death of his family line. Patrick, priggishly, 'developed the ideal that he had made the greatest sacrifice he could in the pursuit of his ambition' in standing against his mother. His training progresses satisfactorily until the girl to whom he was engaged, Nkiru, seduces him by means of a potent charm, becomes pregnant by him, and thus causes him to be banished once and for all from the seminary.

The novel, by its conclusion, seems to imply a triumph of traditional beliefs over new and imported ones in religious matters. Certainly the theme is a fertile one and one that has concerned a number of contemporary African writers – Achebe, Aluko, Soyinka, Ngugi – who explore the possibility of rapprochement between two systems of belief which seem basically incompatible. Nzekwu here does much to make the antagonism which exists between the two systems apparent. Through the statements of Uncle Ononye, perhaps the most convincing character in the novel, we get a clear apprehension of the complicated and sophisticated nature of the family structure of which Patrick becomes the head. The degree of Patrick's responsibility is revealed clearly in this passage:

> Patrick had been spending rather heavily on his relations back home. And rightly too! For, in their traditional social set-up, he occupied the most responsible post of Okpala even though he had not assumed office. The office carried with it the responsibility for the spiritual, mental and physical welfare of the members of the lineage. As Okpala he held in trust for the lineage their religious emblems, landed property, farm lands and other valuables which they inherited from their ancestors. (p. 151)[5]

Uncle Ononye also sums up with precision and intelligence the nature of Christian influence on customary ways and the power of the latter to sustain itself against and benefit from the former, despite the heavy pressures which are brought to bear. It suggests as well that religious influences, and especially the social functions of religion, are central to the total culture and come to bear importantly on most of the functions of that society. The passage is long but worth quoting at length:

> 'Sit down, my boy,' he invited, and Patrick sat close to him. 'You may not know this,' he began, 'but Christianity and our traditional way of life have been in conflict right from the very first day her missionaries stepped on our soil. The Christian missionaries have

always criticised our customs and called us "Bushmen". They have called us "pagans", "heathens", words which I am told mean people without a religion. Yet, in the few months you have been home, you have seen and heard enough to realise that we do have a religion. Mind you, the early missionaries were very nice people, even though they spoke against our ways. I have nothing against them as individuals.

'For many years after they came they offered us the Bible and preached to us about heaven and hell. We found them and their sermons unattractive and boring; but still we went and listened to them because at the end of each religious service or lecture, they distributed dresses, bottles of kerosene, heads of tobacco and items of household use to us.

'We were made. They discovered they could not change us and so they decided to turn their attention to our children, who were yet unformed and pliable, and who would be the fathers of tomorrow. They introduced schools and made them the cover under which Christianity would operate. To my mind, the essential thing to them was not the teaching of reading, writing and arithmetic, which we have now learned to value as the passport to future wealth and power, but the spread of the foreign faith. As soon as the mission hospitals were built even those institutions became a means of spreading the faith. Patients, as long as they could walk, were made to attend religious services morning and evening.

'Because of their avowed policy of using all the means at their disposal – schools and hospitals, which in themselves were very welcome – for the spread of Christianity, they blundered. They sought to change our whole way of living, and in its place to create such conditions as existed in their own country and conducive to the spread of their faith. They refused to realise the degree of influence which our traditional religion has on our environment and which, in turn, is a powerful factor in education. They choose to treat the traditional religion as if it did not exist, despite the fact that every day its role in our lives was being borne in on them.

'I must say it was noble of those who initiated such humanitarian policies and institutions as are those of the Christians! But I maintain that unless their agents have common sense enough to realise that Christianity has to be modified to make it acceptable to us they will make no true converts.' (pp. 86–7)

Here, too, the character has become a *raissoneur* and the speech has the quality of the sermon about it. It is successful to the extent that it presents both sides of the question while displaying a (wholly natural) African bias.

Yet even though passages like this are found in the novel Nzekwu does not take all the opportunities, both intellectually and artistically, that his theme affords. This is so for a number of reasons. The most important of these is that we are never really made aware of the **33** strength of the appeal of Christianity to Patrick, an appeal so strong that it causes him to sacrifice a mother and a way of life. We are told he has the desire but we are not made to feel its force. Achebe, for example, writes of the powerful appeal of Christianity to Nwoye in *Things Fall Apart* as follows:

> It was not the mad logic of the Trinity that captivated him. He did not understand it. It was poetry of the new religion, something felt in the marrow. The hymn about brothers who sat in darkness and in fear seemed to answer a vague and persistent question that haunted his young soul – the question of the twins crying in the bush and the question of Ikemefuna who was killed. He felt a relief within as the hymn poured into his parched soul. The words of the hymn were like the drops of frozen rain melting on the dry palate of the panting earth. Nwoye's callow mind was greatly puzzled.

No corresponding passage is found in *Blade Among the Boys* and the result is that the novel lacks a convincing dramatic centre.

It is true that we feel by implication something of the force of Patrick's convictions in the much anthologised scene where he repudiates his mother. This is a scene (in chapter 15) of great dramatic power. But its convincingness in terms of the logic of the story and plot is mitigated by our recollection that for a long time she supported her son's desire to follow the career she comes to fear. The ambiguities of her position are not resolved when Nzekwu has her say, 'Please. Patrick. This must be the devil's voice that you heard. If God called you, he would have spoken to me, too.' Her twin desires, that her son become a priest and that he, at the same time, continue the patrilineal line, have been incompatible from the outset.

A third factor which weakens the presentation of the problem in the novel is the fact that nowhere is a powerful and convincing missionary point of view presented. The priests who run the Holy Trinity College in Lagos are wholly unsympathetic people. When Patrick raises questions of a pressing religious kind, especially to a boy who seeks to become a priest, he is slapped down. The priests in the seminary which he attends after his brief career with the railroad barely emerge as characters. As we have said, it is natural and right that an African viewpoint should prevail here as in Achebe's or Ngugi's novels. But the strength of this viewpoint would be enhanced and not weakened were the forces with which traditional culture contends made both more explicit and more palpable. This is a less successful novel than the first, I believe, because Patrick is made to stand alone: his values seem idiosyncratic rather than typical, his dilemma isolated from his peers rather than symptomatic of that which concerns them. Such was not the case with Peter Obisie in *Wand of Noble Wood*, the implications of whose dilemma reflected a broad cultural reality.

Moreover there is much extraneous material here which seems to be incorporated so that Nzekwu can display certain features of Nigerian life, interesting enough in themselves, but outside the avowed thematic concern of the book. Nor does the force of the charm which Nkira places on Patrick convince us in the way the *Iyi-ocha* did in the first book. There is much that is valuable in this novel – the evocation of the heterogeneous culture of Kafanchan in the opening chapter where a variety of different peoples are shown to exist in relative harmony as a compelling piece of descriptive writing. The comment made on the way in which the introduction of a cash economy both accounts for the variety of life in the city and promotes the sense of unity which prevails there because all other considerations are secondary to the demands of commerce – this is interesting and valuable comment on a social reality which pervades the country and which is enhanced throughout the book through incidental comments.

The novel is ultimately unsatisfactory because it lacks a strong dramatic centre and a strong central character whose progress in the book rationalises his experiences and gives on them relevance.

In the third novel, *Highlife for Lizards*, we find such a character. This is a very different kind of book, written within more carefully defined limits and much more strict in its precision and control than the earlier novels. It is a domestic novel (in the manner of Flora Nwapa's *Efuru*, Elechi Amadi's *The Concubine*, and Asare Konadu's *A Woman in Her Prime*) set in Iboland in the years between 1912 and 1946. There is as much anthropology in this novel as in the others, though not as much material which is extraneous to the main plot, but here the descriptive element almost wholly gives way to a dramatic treatment. The dramatic treatment is enhanced and supported by an abundance of imagery and metaphor almost wholly lacking in the first two novels, which adds an extra dimension of implication to the story. There is hardly a page in the novel without something in the way of traditional verbal material transmuted by Nzekwu into English. Similarly, there is much more dialogue and less plainly rhetorical monologue than in the earlier books. The reader therefore has a sensation of life in the novel and feels that he is no longer merely a spectator to its action.

Highlife for Lizards tells the story of Agom and her life in Ozoma, one of the six villages which together make up the township of Onitsha. The novel begins, as the prologue tells us, in November 1912, on the day of Agom's wedding to Udesue. Agom is an intelligent, attractive, **35** energetic and independent woman. Her principal concern is to fulfil her obligations as a wife but she engages in trade and creates, as the years pass, a modest fortune for herself. Udezue is not an easy man; he is by turns indolent and energetic and subject to sudden and frequent violent acts against Agom. Of the two, she is the stronger and after a time she endures rather than participates in their marriage. Her child-lessness feeds the antagonism which informs their marriage and Udezue, when Agom visits relatives in Enugu, takes a second wife, Nwadi, a girlhood friend of Agom's and married to one Okoli. Nwadi's presence in the household is ambiguous: she represents both a slight to Agom while at the same time she assists her, and for a time brings peace to the household. Moreover she bears a child by Udezue. But eventually Nwadi proves both incapable and indolent and, when Agom at last has a child, dangerous. Udezue finally drives Mwadi from the house. The last third of the novel then is given over to showing a series of minor events of public importance in which Agom participates – the growth of her businesses, her acquiring titles in the clan, and so on – and all these things against the background of her now happy marriage with Udezue. (This final section of the novel is as loose in structure as the earlier book.) The novel comes to a quiet close and the epilogue – the date is 6 June, 1946 – shows Agom and Udezue discussing the place of man and woman in the home.

The first two parts of the novel – entitled 'The Pot is Broken' and 'A Nudity Show' – are the best parts of the book because the most con-sistently wrought in terms of story and of art. This is so because here Nzekwu is able to work more or less consistently at the level of realism and at the same time at the level of symbolic statement. The prologue prepares us for this. On her wedding night, her husband asleep beside her, Agom hears a cockerel crow:

> Its harsh voice jarred on her nerves and a cool shiver ran down her spine. ... It was taboo, in all the nine villages that made up the riverside town, for a cockerel to crow in the dead of night. When-ever the taboo is broken the offending cockerel met with instant death. For it was believed that its continuing existence would alien-ate the affections of Ani, the earth goddess ... It was particularly annoying that the cockerel had chosen this very night, her home-coming night to break the taboo. To every Onitsha woman her home-coming night was the most sacred in her life. It was the night she made her great sacrifice – her own blood – on the altar of her matri-monial home to gain her heart's most cherished desire – children... In all her years in her father's house she had been brought up to regard these happenings as ill-omens. Her heart told her they added up to no good. Evil lurked somewhere; but where? Afraid, she nudged her husband into wakefulness. (pp. 10–11)[6]

There is, then, the suggestion that there is some force superior to rational apprehension, which will assist in the working out in her life of an insistent fatality. The forewarning of the prologue is reiterated as soon as the proper action of the novel begins, in this form:

> Whenever she dreamt, the dream was a reproduction of some tragic incident from her past. Worse than this, it heralded some unpleasant episode that was to upset the tenor of her family life. Agom hated dreaming; but a dream is indifferent to the feelings of the dreamer, and this dream was another affliction. (p. 15)

And given support throughout the first two parts of the novel by such passages as the following:

> 'There was happiness in our home,' Agom recalled, 'until he became Okpala, priest of the ancestral cult of our patrilineal lineage. I remember the take-over ceremony – I was only eleven then, but I can still remember it vividly – a little unimpressive ceremony that sparked off the series of misfortunes in our home. Two of my brothers died within one week of its performance. Father had forty goats; most of them died then. Chicken death took a heavy toll of the many fowls his wife kept. The crops on his farms failed and land disputes plagued him. By the end of the year, he had almost lost everything. It really looked as if our ancestors had turned their backs on them.

The same is shown in various passages when Nwadi, bitterly jealous of Agom – 'it's always Agom. She is the bone sticking across my throat . . . I must render her ineffective.' – tries various charms to assist her in defeating her rival.

Michael Echeruo, in a review entitled 'Attempting a Ritual Presentation',[7] writes thus of what he conceives of as Nzekwu's principle intention in the novel:

> In *Highlife for Lizards*, Nzekwu seems to me to be willing to attempt a mythic – or at least, a ritual – presentation of the story. He seems willing here, to attempt a larger meaning than would have been possible through the mere facts of his story, however meticulously documented.

Echeruo's review makes much useful comment in support of this contention, through reference to various comments in the novel which evidence 'symbolic' implication: for example, 'To Ofili's telling the tale of the seventh queen who lent her buttocks to a monkey and almost failed to get them back, a tale which finds a parallel in real life, and his **37**

wife, Nwadi, deserts him for Udezue; to Udezue's ritual bathing, etc.'
But Echuruo concludes his discussion by saying:

> In this connection one has to admit that the symbolic possibilities
> which I have indicated to be inherent in Nzekwu's method in the
> novel are not always fully realised. . . . These possibilities of symbolic
> or mythic meaning are not fully realised, it seems to me, because this
> higher purpose is continually being compromised by another ten-
> dency in Nzekwu's fiction – the honest but dangerous desire to indi-
> cate in some detail the facts of the specific cultural, social or historic
> contents of the action and the symbol.

The examples of this that he offers have sometimes to do with aesthetics
– with, for example, a piece of descriptive comment which can mar an
imaginative effect – as when at the end of a description of Agom's
dressing herself for her wedding in the prologue, Nzekwu adds a 'dis-
tracting clinical detail' about a mirror surrounded by a wooden frame
with a handle. This kind of criticism it seems to me is legitimate. But the
second kind of complaint Echeruo offers devolves around the matters of
plot; for example, the information we are given about Agom's leasing
land and involving herself in the palm-oil trade or preparing and selling
illicit gin. Of passages such as this Echeruo says:

> One complains of these weaknesses because one is aware of the im-
> portance of the total novel, and of the dissatisfaction which the
> erring passages contribute. One complains also because the presence
> of these passages is symptomatic of a laxity in construction such as
> often leads to the unimportant and unrewarding developments.

I cite this critique at length because it seems to me that he places undue
emphasis on the mythic or ritual element in the novel. It seems to me
that this is a domestic novel or novel of manners of the kind we defined
above; that this is a novel which creates real people with problems
needing solution, places them in a real world and lets them set about
solving their problems. It sets out, by implication, to suggest answers to
the question 'How do men live?' Agom is not so very different from
Okonkwo in *Things Fall Apart* or Efuru in Flora Nwapa's novel in the
sense that she, like they, is aware that she may well be at the mercy of
an indifferent fate, that religious/magical forces can be operative and
therefore need to be propitiated. Nevertheless, despite the integrity and
the intensity of her awareness, she also knows she must get about the
business of living – and this is what she does.

The climax of the novel is effectively reached when Agom, who despite her helpfulness, goodness, and honesty in her dealings with Nwadi,

is unable to win her affection, sees the latter sent away; then she achieves at last a meaningful relationship with Udezue. Her domestic success assured, Agom now can commit herself to public commercial pursuits. She consolidates her palm-oil trade, she participates in a strike against the colonial government which seeks to interfere with tradition, she assumes the role of priestess of *Isi-ada* – not without some misgivings:

> Agom knew, long before she was called upon officially to the office of priestess, that she was next in line of succession. She knew she could not ignore that call when it came nor could she reject the office. Any such action would be suicidal. Yet she was tormented by doubts as to what her fate would be. Would she continue in her prosperity which derived from a flourishing oil trade? Or would her hands shrink when she assumed office just as her father's had done some twenty-seven years before when he became Okpala, the male counterpart of the office she would soon take over?
>
> Agom searched history and her memory. She studied the fate of all *Isi-ada* she'd known. Only one or two of them had suffered any reverses after assuming office but she had no way of knowing whether these reverses derived from the office. She found herself hoping that the ancestral spirits would spare her the anguish of a declining fortune while she served them. (p. 182)

She becomes a priestess, as well, of Ozoma and such is the strength of her ambition that she says:

> Do you know that if Omu – the traditional queenship – were still in vogue, I would not rest until I got it?

The force of religious belief is still apparent even though domestic affairs predominate in the last section of the novel. This seems to be consistent with the flow and intention of the novel. Agom's story is representative of the careers of many people like herself at this point in time.

The success of the novel turns on a more sustained dramatic treatment. The life of the community in this book is given from the point of view of a participant in that life and not an observer. At the centre is Agom, a consistently engaging character. She has gaiety and warmth and humour, intelligence and shrewdness, and tenacity. She knows to a degree how to accommodate herself to the situations which confront her. She is both conservative and radical: she honours the convention and belief of her forebears and her society, yet her individuality is never compromised and her intelligence, in sway over her emotions, leads her out of the various dilemmas which confront her.

In opposition to Agom are Udezue and Nwadi, both fully-drawn **39** fictional characters, both suitable foils to Agom. Udezue's nature contrasts with Agom's – he has neither the certainty of purpose she possesses nor are his emotions under as strict control. In the early parts of the novel he is capricious, contradictory, and often cruel. He depends on Agom's presence and judgement more than he is prepared to admit and more than she allows herself to show. He must calculate in marrying Nwadi who resembles Agom to the extent that she is singular in her pursuit of her desires but whose motivations, unlike Agom's, are selfish and mean-spirited, and who displays a kind of whining self-pity which is anathema to Agom. In attempting to see the twin marriage safely over the shoals of discontent, Agom allows Udezue to make his own discoveries about Nwadi and in banishing her he restores both his manhood and his marriage.

Nzekwu works mostly at the level of social realism describing the life of his people – their environment, pursuits, customs, idiosyncrasies – he is a writer who in this regard is in the vanguard, along with Achebe, Ekwensi, Aluko, and Flora Nwapa – in initiating a literary tradition which reflects the serious concerns of African peoples, a tradition comprised of writing which reveals a special commitment to formulating the basic values of societies which seeks to 'absorb the best in foreign cultures' whilst retaining 'what is best in our own'.

NOTES

1. Aragbabalu, Omijidi, *Black Orpheus*, No. 11, Mbari, Ibadan, 1960.
2. All quotations in this article are from *Wand of Noble Wood*, London, Hutchinson's edition, first published 1961. Now available in Heinemann African Writers Series.
3. Taiwo, O. *An Introduction to West African Literature*, Nelson, London, 1968.
4. *loc. cit.*
5. All quotations in this article are from *Blade Among the Boys*, London, Hutchinson's edition, first published 1962. Now available in Heinemann African Writers Series.
6. All quotations in this article are from *Highlife for Lizards*, London, Hutchinson's edition, first published 1965.
7. Echeruo Michael, 'Attempting a Ritual Presentation', *Nigeria Magazine*, No. 87 (December 1965), pp. 288–91.

T. M. Aluko: Nigerian Satirist

Bernth Lindfors

Timothy Mofolorunso Aluko is one of the oldest Nigerian writers, in terms of both age and experience.[1] Born in the Yoruba town of Ilesha in 1918, he was educated at schools in Western Nigeria and received professional training in civil engineering and town planning at Yaba Higher College in Lagos and at the University of London. When he returned to Nigeria in 1950, he took a position as an engineer in the Public Works Department. In 1956 he was appointed Town Engineer to the Lagos Town Council and in 1960 Director of Public Works for Western Nigeria. Today he teaches at the University of Ife.

According to the blurb on the dust jacket of his first novel, Aluko 'was first encouraged to write fiction by F. N. Williams, first Representative of the British Council in Nigeria. He won prizes in short story writing contests organised by the British Council in Nigeria in 1944 and 1945, and did writing as a hobby during his student days in Britain (1946–1950).'[2] In the late nineteen-forties and early fifties a number of his short stories and articles were published in the *West African Review*[3] and broadcast by the BBC African Service.[4] Aluko's writing career thus began very much as Cyprian Ekwensi's did a few years later.

Ekwensi, of course, soon overtook him. It is rather difficult to determine exactly when Aluko wrote his first novel *One Man, One Wife*, but it did not appear until 1959, five years after *People of the City*. And unlike every Nigerian novel before and since, it was published in Lagos rather than London – an indication, perhaps, that it was unacceptable to British publishers.

One Man, One Wife[5] is a garbled tale about polygamy and church politics in a newly Christianised society. Elder Joshua, a recent convert, is distressed when he learns that the new religion forbids him to marry a second wife, for he has already paid the bride price on a preadolescent girl named Toro. To save himself embarrassment and money, he plans to marry Toro off to his grown son Jacob, but Jacob refuses to go along with the idea, insisting that he needs a marriageable girl right away. Joshua then arranges for him to wed Joke who, four days after the marriage, proves to be pregnant by another man. From this interesting beginning the novel deteriorates into chaos and confusion. Joke and Joshua die, and the focus of the story shifts to Royanson, an expelled church member who has set himself up as a 'Public Letter Writer and Notary, Friend of the Illiterate, Advocate of the Oppressed.'[6] Because he is one of the few educated men in the village, Royanson earns a very comfortable living writing letters in English for illiterate tribesmen who want to make their legal and personal grievances known to European officials in the government. Eventually he goes mad, and Jacob and Toro are brought back to the centre of the stage to finish out the story. The last twenty-five pages describe a smallpox epidemic, a court case, a suicide, and a sudden religious conversion, all rather clumsily contrived episodes in a wildly meandering plot.

The only redeeming features of the novel are Aluko's occasional flashes of wit and satire. He pokes fun at the old order as well as the new, sometimes ridiculing them both in the same breath. At a meeting of tribal elders the conflict between traditional and western beliefs is brought out in a humorous fashion:

Bada then pointed out another menace of Christianity in the village. The Christians, led by the pastor from Idasa and Bible Jeremiah, had been trying to dissuade the villagers from worshipping the mighty Shonponna ... That was a flagrant affront to the might and majesty of the god of smallpox. Bada, son of Ogunmodede and High Priest of Shonponna, was warning the Asolo that unless Bible Jeremiah and his mad Christian followers cleared out of the village, Shonponna would surely visit Isolo with a terrible epidemic of smallpox in the next dry season ... Shonponna, M'lord of smallpox, was a very jealous god. The villagers could not be too careful about him. But the White Man had shown some bias towards the new religion. In fact, it had been rumoured that it came from the White Man's country, and that it was his religion. In that case the villagers could not drive away the village Christians without exposing themselves to the White Man's anger.

'These are serious words. Elders of Isolo, what shall we do?' The Asolo of Isolo repeated his worried question.

Chief Lotun slumbered in reply. (pp. 99–100)

Aluko is also capable of launching direct attacks upon native institutions and customs. Here is his description of what is traditionally done with headstrong girls who violate marriage contracts made for them by their parents:

A daughter who refused to marry the suitor of her parent's choosing was invariably sent to the Oba's palace. There she regretted her folly at leisure. A queen. But what a queen! A new member of the large harem, she would be attached as a ward to an elderly wife for whom she slaved as a domestic servant while she learnt in return the endless tradition, rites and don'ts that went with life in the palace. The new bride was one of scores in the same unenviable position of sharing in common the hand of an indolent old potentate. The number of his women he could never tell. Indeed, most of the queens in the palace were the mistresses of the Oba's elder sons, relatives and hangers-on. A queen of the palace – ah what a queen! (p. 108)

It is in his attitude towards the past that Aluko differs most from nostalgic novelists like Chinua Achebe and his school of Ibo followers. Aluko sees nothing noble or dignified about traditional tribal life. He laughs at the villagers who worship gods of lightning, iron and small-pox, and the priests of these gods are invariably exposed as hypocrites and charlatans who prey on the superstitious fears of their neighbours. Traditional rulers like the Oba and village chiefs are portrayed as indolent, self-serving rogues more interested in preserving their powers and privileges than in wisely governing their people. As Arthur Drayton has aptly noted:

[Aluko] has attempted to do for Yorubaland what [Achebe] has done for Iboland, namely to present an image of the past at that point where the civilisation of the Western world came into contact with it. But whereas Mr Achebe assesses the two civilisations objectively, writing from the inside at the same time, Mr Aluko attitudinises and, what is more, does on the whole lack that empathy which is so necessary if a historical novel is to rise above the level of bald observation. The result is that the novel convinces only in patches, and that his interpretation of the past appears to suffer from bias and preconceptions. His is almost a total rejection of the past.[7] **43**

Aluko also rejects the present. The tribesmen who convert to Christianity and western ways are certainly no holier than their pagan kinsmen. Church elders, for example, quarrel and manoeuvre for high position just as aspirants for chiefly titles do. And western education does nothing to improve the character of individuals like Royanson, the money-hungry letter writer. Indeed, Aluko's view of mankind appears to be a rather pessimistic one. He seems to feel that although human institutions and manners change as the old order gives way to the new, man remains the imperfect, foolish, corrupt creature he has always been. To Aluko this is not tragic but funny. Aluko does not share Achebe's gloom.

Nor does he share Achebe's sensitivity to language. Instead of attempting to simulate African vernacular in dialogue and narration, Aluko writes in a very Anglicised style. At times the African milieu is totally obliterated, as in these lines from a folktale told by one of his characters: 'Nikun was the most beautiful damsel on earth. Her hair was of black silk; her teeth were as white as snow and looked like pearls.' (p. 25) Damsel, silk, snow, pearls – these are hardly the words an African raconteur would use to tell an African tale to an African audience. Nor would a Yoruba ordinarily refer to a body wrapper as a 'sarong' or address any of his gods as 'm'lord'.[8] When Aluko has his characters speak or write English, he sometimes satirises the bombast employed by the semi-educated African. A typical letter to the editor of a Nigerian newspaper begins:

> Sir,
>   Permit me a space in your widely and voraciously read journal to bring to the notice of the readers of your most widely read and voraciously digested newspaper domiciled in this great dependency of Nigeria some curious and wonderfully strange incidents and events that have been transpiring and occurring in one village in the District of Idasa, to wit Isolo. (p. 123)

This is good fun, but Aluko does not know how to use such techniques in moderation. Bombast becomes letter-writer Royanson's characteristic mode of expression, whether he is speaking in English or Yoruba, and the reader quickly tires of it. Aluko also occasionally intrudes to address the reader directly ('What happened in the room? Come, come, ask another, you simpleton!' p. 138) or to exhort one of his characters in a biblical idiom:

> Why criest thou, woman? Why art thou forlorn? Why art thou sore distressed, woman? Why puttest thou thy trust in the White Man's

magic, that was not known to thy father? Go hence to thy village, Isolo. Go hence to thy mother's god, the great Shonponna that slayeth by the hundreds. He knoweth thy trouble, and can find thee thy missing daughter. Still tarriest thou, woman? (p. 157)

This too becomes tiresome when over used.[9] In style as well as structure and message, *One Man, One Wife* is far too erratic and undisciplined to be a satisfying novel.

Aluko's second novel *One Man, One Matchet*[10] was only a moderate improvement on his first. Published in London as late as 1964, it could easily have been influenced by Achebe's first two novels but apparently was not. Aluko's illiterate African characters still spoke like tribalised Englishmen with no knowledge of African proverbs, metaphors, or figures of speech, and his plot structure remained loose and episodic. He did succeed in dramatising events more effectively than before and in giving his satirical thrusts sharper point, but his story was little more than a clumsy patchwork of contiguous incidents, some interesting, some not.

Most of the incidents centre on the activities of Benjamin Benjamin, an ill-educated politician and journalist who makes trouble for a newly-appointed African District Officer by encouraging his people to refuse to pay taxes and to oppose government measures to cut down diseased cocoa trees in the district. At the same time he exploits his people by collecting huge sums of money from them to be used, he says, for paying legal expenses in court cases which will benefit the district. Most of the money he collects goes into his own pocket. For a while Benjamin Benjamin succeeds in thwarting the government and in fattening his purse, but when his leadership results in bloodshed and rioting, he is killed by one of his own followers.

Though 'Benja-Benja', as the villagers call him, is the liveliest character in the novel, Aluko's hero is really Udo Akpan, the African District Officer who labours to undo the damage done by the rogue-politician. An idealistic young man, Akpan is distrusted by the villagers because he occupies a white man's post and refuses to take bribes. He rapidly gains a reputation as a 'black white man' who sides with the colonial government instead of with his own people. This is culture conflict with a new twist. Unlike Obi Okonkwo, Patrick Ikenga and other westernised heroes who suffer because they want to break away from the tribe and its traditions, Udo Akpan suffers because he is unable to gain acceptance in traditional society. In seeking to establish rapport with the villagers whose district he administers, he must continually do battle with a corrupt, semi-westernised African politician who has already won their confidence and is exploiting it for his own selfish ends. Akpan's **45** efforts to create a working relationship with the tribe are also sporadically frustrated by the inefficient bureaucratic system Nigeria has inherited from Britain. In other words, he is foiled more often by western forces than by traditional forces. He does not triumph over Benjamin Benjamin; he merely outlasts him. And in the final chapter he has not yet found a satisfactory way to introduce innovation and progress to a tradition-bound African society.

The novel touches on many topical Nigerian problems – exploitation of the uneducated by the educated, political irresponsibility, bribery, misappropriation of public funds – but it fails to make a forceful, cohesive statement about Nigerian experience. The story is so cluttered with unimportant incidents that it loses clear focus, and the characters, never adequately individualised in speech or action, remain lifeless and lost in the haze. The best scenes are those in which Benjamin Benjamin is perpetrating yet another fraud upon his unsuspecting kinsmen. The worst are those in which Aluko baldly editorialises on the action by setting up artificial conversations in the manner of Nzekwu in order to discuss important issues. In such scenes all momentum is lost. Benjamin Benjamin, the only interesting character, is not strong enough to carry the dead weight of the novel by himself.

Fortunately, a number of passages are enlivened by Aluko's spirited sense of humour. He is particularly adept at parody and burlesque and very tellingly mimics the tone and idiom of demagogic political oratory, inflammatory newspaper editorials, wordy civil service directives, and zealous church prayers. At one point Benjamin Benjamin delivers a funeral oration in the style of the Gettysburg Address, urging his fellow mourners to 'here highly resolve that this honoured dead shall not have died in vain, that this ancient city of Ipaja under God shall have a new birth of freedom, and that government of the people of Ipaja by the people of Ipaja for the people of Ipaja shall not perish from the earth.' (p. 114) Aluko's cleverness at imitating the pretentious speech of his uneducated countrymen adds greater satirical bite to his fiction, giving it extra moral as well as comic force.

Nevertheless, *One Man, One Matchet* remains in too many ways a repeat of *One Man, One Wife*. Aluko has changed some of his targets but few of his techniques, and the result is another rambling, episodic farce told in a language which fails to evoke the appropriate African milieu. On occasion Aluko repeats himself virtually verbatim. Here is a scene from *One Man, One Wife* in which an illiterate elder thanks an educated young man for reading a letter aloud to him:

46   'My son, Jacob, sat at one end, many days' march away. He wrote something on these papers. . . . Then someone came along and delivered this to me, saying that it is a message from my son, Jacob. Now you were not there when he wrote this letter . . . I brought this envelope to you . . . and you read it. You make me feel as if my son himself sits there in the chair speaking to me. This is wonderful. . . . This is the White Man's magic.' (p. 36)

In *One Man, One Matchet* one finds a very similar scene:

'My son wrote on a a piece of paper a long, long way away. The paper is brought here. You were not there when the paper was written by my son. Yet you here read the words of my son from this paper. That is wisdom. It is magic. White Man's magic.' (p. 70)

Obviously Aluko was still relying very heavily upon his own resources and not paying too much attention to what other Nigerian novelists were doing.

In his third novel, *Kinsman and Foreman*,[11] Aluko took up another familiar theme in West African fiction: the return of the 'been-to'. When Titus Oti returns from London as the first professionally qualified Nigerian civil engineer to join the Public Works Department, he is made District Engineer of Ibala, his home town. This unfortunate posting leaves him prey to his relatives and to the local church which expects generous financial contributions from him. Worse still, he soon discovers that Simeon Oke, his kinsman and a foreman in the PWD, is totally corrupt. Should he bring charges against his kinsman? Titus is spared answering this question when another man hauls Simeon to court for dishonest practices. After a lengthy trial Simeon is acquitted on a technicality. Titus Oti's troubles are over when Simeon is transferred to a different region.

There is not much difference between the situation in this novel and the situation in *One Man, One Matchet*; an honest man and a rogue are in conflict, and the rogue eventually loses out. What gives *Kinsman and Foreman* an interesting twist is the family connection between the honest man and the rogue. This connection puts a great deal of strain on Titus, who must decide whether to be loyal to his conscience or to his kinsman. Although Aluko allows Titus to agonise over this question for a while, he never allows him to make a decision. Another character is brought in to initiate legal proceedings against Simeon, and Titus is made to fall mysteriously ill during the trial so he can't even be called upon to testify against his kinsman. By these rather clumsy devices Aluko manages to sidestep the moral and psychological problems inherent in the situation he has created. Had he chosen instead to face up to these problems, Titus might have achieved significant heroic stature **47** and *Kinsman and Foreman* might have become something more than a rather frivolous comedy.

Nevertheless, taken for what it is, this novel has several good points. First, unlike Aluko's other novels, it is well organised. Amusing incidents are skilfully strung together and knotted at the end into a hilarious climax. The narrative moves along unfettered by the irrelevancies and digressions that crippled the earlier novels. Secondly, the characters are quite well-defined, with each one having a special role to play in the parade of comic events. In addition, Aluko's satirical thrusts are more widely distributed than in his previous novels. He slashes with vigour at church, state, family and individual. Even the follies of British justice and American philanthropy receive a few pertinent jabs. If one compares *Kinsman and Foreman* with Aluko's formless first novel published only seven years earlier, one can see quite clearly that Aluko has come a long way in a short time. He still has a good distance to go before he will be close to front-runners, but he is moving in the right direction.

There are interesting similarities between Aluko's last work and some of Achebe's which lead one to wonder whether Achebe has influenced Aluko. Oti's situation in *Kinsman and Foreman* is not unlike Obi Okonkwo's in *No Longer at Ease*, though the two heroes come to very different ends. Both novels provide a close-up view of corruption in the Nigerian civil service and of the social pressures which encourage new civil servants to conform to the pattern of public exploitation established by their peers and predecessors. Aluko dodges some of the issues that Achebe tackles with vigour, but he does come out rather strongly in favour of social reform. Both authors use satire very effectively, and Aluko, for the first time in his fiction, writes bits of dialogue in an African vernacular style. Here is how an old man introduces Titus to Simeon in the opening pages of the novel:

'Simeon, this is Titus the son of your kinsman Samuel, now gone to heaven. I hand him to you this day as your own son. You are to direct his going out and his coming in in the PWD. You know all the intricacies of Government work. Titus has only the book knowledge of Government work: he does not know the other side. You know it. If the railway train runs non-stop for a hundred years, will it not always find that land is still ahead of it? If a child boasts that he has as many clothes as his father, can he equally boast of having as many rags as his father?

'And you, Titus, you must listen to the words of my mouth. Where Simeon tells you to go, you must go. Where he tells you there is no way, know there is no way; turn back. Associate with the men he tells you are safe. Avoid those he points out to you as dangerous. Let the eyes of Simeon be your eyes from this day on; let his hands be your hands. Does the thread not follow the path made by the needle?

'It is in spite of the snake that the bush rat nurtures its young to maturity. Regardless of the activities of human snakes, you Simeon will pilot your child Titus to success in Government work.' (pp. 6–7)

Aluko does not use this technique as often or as successfully as Achebe, but the fact that he uses it at all is a sure indication that he has recognised the potential of a vernacular register.

Aluko's debt to Achebe is even more apparent in his fourth novel *Chief the Honourable Minister*,[12] which reverberates with direct and indirect echoes from *A Man of the People*. It tells the story of Alade Moses, a school principal who has been appointed Minister of Works in the corrupt government of Afromacoland. Like Nanga, Moses luxuriates in plush offices and regal living quarters, and he is married to an uneducated woman whom he considers beneath his station in life.

Everyone that had eyes to see knew that Bose was not beautiful and that she was not a wife that the headmaster of a grammar school would be encouraged to introduce to his friends. It was obvious that she was going to become an even greater embarrassment to him now that he had become a Minister. (p.19)

So Moses takes up with a pretty young nurse who is happy to serve as both his mistress and confidante. There his resemblance to Nanga ends, for unlike most other ministers in Afromacoland, he is neither a full-time womaniser nor a fool. Indeed, in some ways he appears to be more closely akin to confused idealists such as Achebe's Odili and Obi Okonkwo. His remarkable academic career and solid reputation as a headmaster have made him the most respected citizen in the village of Newtown, and his people pressure him into politics because they want their village to be represented in parliament by its most eminent and distinguished son. Though Moses would much rather spend his life leading his people out of a wilderness of ignorance than into a promised land of milk and money, he consents to be guided by their desires and to run for office. Soon he is known as Chief the Honourable Alade Moses, MP, BA (Hons.), Dip. Ed., Minister of Works, the Asiwaju of Newtown.

The crux of his problem turns out to be that he is an honest man thrust into an intrinsically dishonest position. He is surrounded by corrupt underlings who have a vested interest in keeping him in power in order to exploit the prestige and prerogatives of his office. These unscrupulous lieutenants do not hesitate to rig elections, bribe officials **49** and extort government funds on his behalf. Two of them, an old chief and a young Secretary General of the Newtown Improvement Union named Gorgeous Gregory, even go so far as to coerce illiterate towns-people to swear a tribal oath that they will vote for Moses in a forth-coming election. It is not surprising that in the turmoil following the election, Moses is one of the government ministers set upon and killed by rampaging crowds. The novel ends, as *A Man of the People* and so many other African novels do nowadays with a military coup which restores order to a society that has been debauched by its politicians.

Aluko appears to want us to believe that Moses was a good man overwhelmed by forces of evil he could neither restrain nor suppress. But too often he seems to be little more than a floating jellyfish – weak, passive and morally flabby. Though his conscience bothers him when he discovers what his subordinates and colleagues in government are up to, he never takes decisive action to oppose their schemes. His conduct, in office and out, is based on convenience not principle. At one point he reflects on his unhappy position:

> Long after Gorgeous Gregory had gone, Moses sat in his chair in the lounge thoroughly displeased with himself. Again the thought came to him for the umpteenth time that he must take a stand somewhere. There must be a limit to the dishonourable acts that he would allow his name to be associated with. But again for the umpteenth time the realisation came to him that his action was now ill-timed and belated. (p. 181)

Moses continues to postpone taking 'ill-timed and belated' moral stands until it seems he has no morals left to stand on. Others take advantage of his spinelessness, forcing him into such degraded postures that he loses all reputation for integrity. 'What could be responsible for his rapid deterioration?' one of the characters in the novel asks, and the reader is tempted to answer 'abnormal frailty'.

For Moses, like nearly all Aluko's heroes, displays a marked reluc-tance to take any responsible action that might be unpopular with his people. He would rather follow them into a familiar rut that he knows to be wrong than attempt to lead them in a new direction that he feels is right. Aluko's attitude appears to be that it would be foolish for men like Moses to try to initiate reforms when so many of their fellows are con-tent with things as they are. In such a world it does not pay to be too serious about matters of principle. One should laugh, not weep, at the follies of man. This kind of jovial pessimism borders on deep cyni-cism.

50   Aluko's intention, of course, is satire, and frequent use of mordant irony often helps him to achieve his ends. One reason Moses fails, we are told, is because he is a man out of his element; had he been minister of something he understood, like education, he might at least have succeeded in remaining honest. That post, however, has been awarded to an ill-educated party hack who was as poorly equipped to handle his duties as Moses was to cope with the taxing demands made on the integrity of a Minister of Works. Indeed, the only government employees who seem to really know how to do their work properly are the British expatriate civil servants, and they are so efficient that several cabinet ministers recommend they be sacked as saboteurs. Their only treasonable offence is that they do their jobs too well. Such are the absurdities that Aluko delights in holding up to ridicule and scorn. Because he has a keen eye for human fatuity, an alert ear for hypocrisy, and a fine but cutting comic touch, his satire, when good, is very, very good.

But when bad, it can be horrid. For instance, he never tires of calling the lecherous Minister of Education a 'Minister of Ladies' or of showing how much time is wasted at cabinet meetings on trivial and vulgar affairs. Important deliberations are constantly interrupted by foolish telephone calls, and high state officials are always falling asleep on the job, even at public ceremonies. These jokes are funny the first time they occur, but like so much else in Aluko's fiction, they become tedious when repeated too frequently. Aluko has yet to learn to purge his writing of such excesses.

Another annoyance is his style, which is almost unremittingly Anglophonic in rhythm and imagery. Here, for example, is the way Moses addresses his people at a political rally:

> If our critics thought that our government – this government of our people by our people for our people – was going to build the super-structure of our great educational edifice on the shaky foundation left by our colonial masters, then let them think again. We tell them that we know better than to put new wine in old bottles. We will have nothing to do with any foundation that bears any element whatsoever of our unedifying past – a past that we must forget in double quick time. (pp. 130–31)

This amusing parody of stale political rhetoric may actually be a fairly accurate transcription of a certain brand of Nigerian soapbox oratory in English, but it is hardly convincing to have Moses speak in this idiom in discussions with his mistress or with illiterate villagers who purportedly address him in a vernacular language. Aluko does individualise the speech of a few of his rustic characters but he does not **51** work as conscientiously at Africanising his style as he did in *Kinsman and Foreman*. Instead, he appears to have unwittingly lapsed back into his old colonial habits of expression. The stylistic lesson he learned from Achebe now seems to have been all but forgotten.

Although his twenty-five year literary career has been marked by slow, steady artistic progress, it is doubtful whether Aluko will ever write a masterpiece. He is a facile and witty satirist but little beyond that. One searches his novels in vain for the high moral seriousness that pervades even the earliest works of committed artists such as Achebe, Soyinka and Armah. Aluko seems content to merely laugh at his world, and because his laughter contains no undertones of anguish or outrage, it rings hollow. He is a critic without a troubled conscience, a trickling gadfly without a sting. It is the superficiality of his social protest, not the occasional clumsiness of his craftsmanship, that identifies him as a second-rate writer. It is hard to take such a light-hearted comedian seriously.

NOTES

1. Aluko was contributing short stories to the *West African Review* in the late nineteen-forties, long before most Nigerian novelists started writing fiction. Cyprian Ekwensi was the only other novelist to publish short stories this early.
2. Information from the back of the dust jacket of *One Man, One Wife* (Lagos, 1959).
3. His early stories include: 'Strange Captain of the North', *West African Review*, April 1948, pp. 393–95; 'No Welcome for the Ghost', *West African Review*, January 1949, pp. 43f.; 'Art of Dentistry', *West African Review*, October 1949, pp. 1141f.; 'Silence in Court!', *West African Review*, October 1953, pp. 1097f. He also had a story in T. Cullen Young's anthology, *African New Writing* (London 1947), and he wrote a few articles: 'Case for Fiction', *West African Review*, November 1949, pp. 1237f.; 'Polygamy and the Surplus Women', *West African Review*, March 1950, pp. 259–60.
4. Information from the inside flap of the dust jacket of *One Man, One Matchet* (London, Heinemann African Writers Series, 1964).
5. *One Man, One Wife* (Lagos, 1959). All quotations are taken from this edition. A revised edition was published in the Heinemann African Writers Series (London) in 1967.
6. p. 91. The same character type appears in one of Aluko's early stories, 'No Welcome for the Ghost', *West African Review*, January 1949, p. 43.
7. Arthur D. Drayton, 'The Return to the Past in the Nigerian Novel', *Ibadan*, No. 10 (1960), p. 29.

8. See the comments of Ulli Beier, 'Nigerian Literature', *Nigeria Magazine*, No. 66 (October 1960), p. 215.

9. See, e.g., pp. 154, 161.

10. *One Man, One Matchet* (London, Heinemann African Writers Series, 1964). Here, and subsequently, all quotations are taken from the edition cited.

11. *Kinsman and Foreman* (London, Heinemann African Writers Series, 1966).

12. *Chief the Honourable Minister* (London, Heinemann African Writers Series, 1970).

Religion and Life in James Ngugi's *The River Between*

Lloyd Williams

It is the purpose of this paper to bring into focus what I consider to be a very profound theme developed by James Ngugi in his novel, *The River Between*. I am concerned here with Mr Ngugi's consistent statement on life and religion. He knows that religion can be meaningful to a people only if it relates to them in their daily lives, only if it rises out of the important aspects of their past and speaks directly to their experiences in the present. A religion which speaks only of religious ideals and moral truths, without touching on the concrete situation of man in his everyday life, can give to man nothing but emptiness. Specifically, Ngugi is concerned in *The River Between* with the Gikuyu people of Kenya, and with Christianity. He is very consciously aware of how meaningful the Christian faith can be for the Gikuyu people, but he knows that it can be so only as it grows out of their own life situation, *not* as it is imposed upon them from above by the white man as law.

James Ngugi expresses in *The River Between* a line of thought which is dealt with in depth by two theologians, Dr Amos Wilder, Professor of Theology at the Chicago Theological Seminary, and the great, late Dr **54** Paul Tillich, former Professor of Philosophical Theology at Harvard. In

Otherworldliness and the New Testament, Wilder concerns himself with the place of Christianity in the modern world; with the question of how the Christian message can be made relevant to the modern man. Dr Tillich's work, *The Shaking of the Foundations*, deals with the burden of the 'religious law'. The parallels between the theme developed by James Ngugi in *The River Between* and the ideas of Dr Wilder and Dr Tillich as presented in the two above-mentioned works are striking, and my paper will be structured in the form of a parallel comparison.

Amos Wilder is troubled by the fact that so many men do not find their needs met and do not find themselves spoken to by the message of the Bible. He identifies the problem as being that man has succeeded in isolating religion from life. 'In various ways we have separated faith from life and made that faith unreal.' (Wilder, p. 20) He writes that the one great and telling accusation which can be brought against Christianity is that, in the form in which it is so often presented, it evades responsibility for the problems of our life in this world. '. . . the Gospel as it is offered is unreal and irrelevant.' (Wilder, p. 19) Wilder asked: how can religion conserve and renew its essential powers unless it copes with the whole man and with the whole of life? 'It flourishes only as it encounters man where he is and lives'. (p. 23–4) James Ngugi, too, is aware that Christianity must encounter man where he is and lives, that it can be a meaningful faith only as it comes to man within the context of his life in the world. He expresses this awareness through the character of Muthoni. Muthoni has just made clear to her sister Nyambura her wish to be circumcised against their father's will. To Nyambura's shock and surprise Muthoni replies:

> 'Why! Are we fools? . . . Father and mother are circumcised. Are they not Christians? Circumcision did not prevent them from being Christians. I too have embraced the white man's faith. However, I know it is beautiful, oh so beautiful to be initiated into womanhood. You learn the ways of the tribe. Yes, the white man's God does not quite satisfy me. I want, I need something more. My life and your life are here, in the hills, that you and I know.' (*The River Between*, p. 30)[1]

Muthoni knows that religion in and for itself is nothing. She says that she is a Christian. She does not wish to leave the faith. But she realises that her life is inseparably bound up in the ways and life of the tribe, and that Christianity cannot be meaningful to her if it attempts to meet her outside the tribe, outside of her life in the tribe. She tries to explain this to Waiyaki when he questions her as to why she rebelled against her faith:

'No one will understand. I say I am a Christian and my father and **55** mother have followed the new faith. I have not run away from that. But I also want to be initiated into the ways of the tribe ... How could I be outside the tribe, when all the girls born with me at the same time have left me?' (pp. 50–51)

What Muthoni wants is both Christianity and the tribe. She wants to unite the two; she needs religion but knows that Christianity can meet that need only if it comes to her through the idiom of her way of life. Her desire to unite the two forces finds expression in her simple words to Nyambura:

'I am still a Christian, see, a Christian in the tribe . . .' (p. 61)

This central idea of uniting Christianity and the people's way of life can be seen further in the thought of Waiyaki's father, Chege:

Makuyu was now the home of the Christians while Kameno remained the home of all that was beautiful in the tribe. Who would ever bring them together? (p. 63)

and in the figure of Waiyaki himself:

Muthoni had tried. Hers was a search for salvation for herself. She had the courage to attempt a reconciliation of the many forces that wanted to control her. She had realized her need, the need to have a wholesome and beautiful life that enriched you and made you grow. His father, too, had tried to reconcile the two ways, not in himself, but through his son. Waiyaki was the product of that attempt. (p. 163)

Ngugi clarifies this further:

Waiyaki did not like being identified with either side; he was now committed to reconciliation. (p. 125)

Amos Wilder continues with the development of his thesis:

We connect God with our religious ideals and sentiments, and feelings, and overlook the importance for him of those deep dynamic impulses, drives, instincts which come into play in our everyday secular lives. But this means that our Christian life loses power. Its taproots are cut. We forget that grace and revelation come to man not through their heads and hearts, but through the elemental factors in their human nature, through the commonplace but fateful aspects of our mortality . . . (Wilder, p. 21)

56 Wilder argues that a man's real religion or irreligion develops out of his experience with things that are truly important to him as he becomes of age: such as his tension with his elders, achieving acceptance with his fellows, etc. It is in the wrestling with such dilemmas that Wilder believes man has the best chance to discover God, whether in success or failure. Wilder looks to the Bible for support:

> In the Old Testament we see God at work as man seeks to solve his basic problems of family and social life . . . Religion here, as it ought to be with us, wrestles with the powerful, intractable but God-given raw material of human nature as it evolves new patterns in the family and the tribe and the nation. (pp. 31–32)

Wilder takes for illustration the oldest strata of the Old Testament. Here he finds 'a wealth of poignant and often shocking stories about the ABC's of human nature': The episode of Isaac and Abraham – father and son; of Hagar and Ishmael – mother and child. The recognition scene between Joseph and his brethren – brother and brothers; David and Jonathan – comrade and comrade; David and his mighty men – chieftain and followers. Wilder asks why this kind of material is here in such abundance, and concludes that it is because the Bible recognises that God finds his way to us, and we to him, through the commonplace but personally crucial relationships and experiences of life. 'Here we find the raw material of revelations'. (p. 33) Wilder has developed in these passages one essential point: grace, revelation, the word of God, understanding, meaning – whatever term one may wish to use – these reach man through his wrestling with very basic and ordinary experience. James Ngugi makes precisely the same point in *The River Between*. He writes of Waiyaki's memory of Muthoni's last hours:

> She did not last many hours after they arrived in Siriana. Waiyaki could still remember her last words as they approached the hospital. 'Waiyaki,' she turned to him, 'tell Nyambura I see Jesus. And I am a woman, beautiful in the tribe . . .' (*The River Between*, p. 61)

Muthoni has seen Jesus, she has experienced a revelation through the act of her circumcision, a commonplace event in the life of the tribe, yet one which is of crucial importance to Muthoni as an individual. Revelation came to her as she took part in an event which was important to her. Nyambura realises this, and through her reflections on Muthoni's end we see again Ngugi's own expression of the understanding reached and stated directly by Amos Wilder:

> Muthoni said she had seen Jesus. She had done so by going back to the tribe, by marrying the rituals of the tribe with Christ. (pp. 117–18)   **57**

Amos Wilder condemns ministers and preachers who cling to religious ideals and abstracts, who speak of promised ultimate spiritual goals and whose words fail to touch man 'at the level where he has been seared or terrified or haunted'. James Ngugi portrays the character of Joshua as just such a preacher. Joshua addresses his congregation:

> . . . And coming to the New Testament, the Testament that you hold in your hands today, we read, 'And Jesus said "Seek ye first the Kingdom of God" . . .' Therefore, brothers and sisters, I tell you today, come to Jesus. Stand by him. You see him being taken to the Cross. Are you going to desert him? Are you going to deny him like Peter? Remember life here on earth is one of trials, and of hardships. Satan will come to you at night, in your own house, in your field, or even in church here, and he will whisper to you, calling you back to the old ways. 'Njoroge and Joshua,' he will say, 'follow me. This broad and easy road you see here, this, my son, is the right way.' Remember do not hearken to that voice. Let us march with one heart to the new Jerusalem. (p. 98)

Joshua goes on to speak of the faithful and happy band of pilgrims who will remain on the path of righteousness, braving all hardships and thereby qualifying themselves for entrance into the 'Father's mansion', the place which God prepares for the faithful. Wilder writes, 'So it is with many Christians. . . . they live off of ideals and dreams which have very little to do with the rich soil and humus of everyday life'. (p. 67) Satan, the Kingdom of God, the new Jerusalem, 'Stand by Christ's cross' – what do any of these ideals and abstracts spoken of by Joshua have to do with the concrete problems of the people's immediate experiences? Nothing at all. Waiyaki realises the meaninglessness of such preoccupation with religious ideals and through him can be seen Mr Ngugi's condemnation of religion which clings to ultimate spiritual securities; of religion which is divorced from a people's way of life. Waiyaki reflects on Christianity:

> But the religion, the faith, needed washing, cleansing away all the dirt and leaving only the eternal. And that eternal that was the truth had to be reconciled to the traditions of the people. A people's traditions could not be swept away overnight. That way lay disintegration. Such a tribe would have no roots for a people's roots were in their traditions going back to the past, the very beginning, Gikuyu and Mumbi. A religion that did not recognise spots of beauty and truths in their way of life, was useless. It would not satisfy. It would not be a living experience, a source of life and vitality. It would only maim a man's soul, making him cling to whatever promised security, otherwise he would be lost. Perhaps that was what was wrong with Joshua. (p. 162)

In Joshua, Waiyaki sees a man with no roots, a man whose traditions have been swept out from under him leaving him with nothing to hang on to but an abstract ideal, a religious dream – Joshua's new Jerusalem. Joshua, indeed, clings to this ideal with all his might; he becomes obsessed by the dream. Ngugi shows this obsession through Joshua's reflection on circumcision:

> For Joshua indulging in this ceremony was the unforgivable sin. Had he not been told to take up everything and leave Egypt? He would journey courageously, a Christian soldier going on to the promised land. Nobody would deflect him from his set purpose. He wanted to enter the new Jerusalem a whole man. (p. 35)

and again through his thoughts about his daughters' rebellion:

> All right. Let her go back to Egypt. Yes. Let her go back. He, Joshua, would travel on, on to the new Jerusalem. (p. 42)

Amos Wilder and James Ngugi both realise that religion can be a forceful and meaningful part of man's life only if it meets man in his many-sided actualities, only if it comes to him within the context of all the diverse relationships in which he involves himself throughout his life in the world. Speaking to the Christian who has become disillusioned about his faith, Wilder writes:

> You are quite right in looking askance at any self-styled religion that only plays around the edges, that only concerns itself with your soul or your emotions or your capacity for mysticism, or even your troubled conscience. Religion is supposed to do more than any of these things; it is supposed to save! You are quite right in your demand that religion should take over the total situation in which you find yourself. To 'save' means saving the whole-man and not just his emotions. And it cannot be just an individual. The man must be saved in his relationship'. (p. 62)

James Ngugi makes the same point – that religion must come to man within his relationships – through the character of Nyambura who applies the thought behind Wilder's words to her own immediate situation:

> Day by day she was becoming weary of Joshua's brand of religion. Was she too becoming a rebel? No, she would not do as her sister had done. She knew, however, that she had to have a God who would give her a fullness of life, a God who would still her restless soul, so she clung to Christ because he had died on the tree, love for all the people **59**

blazing out from his sad eyes. She wished he could be near her so that she might wash and dress his wounds . . . She prayed to Him. He must not leave her. Even this did not always satisfy her and she hungered for someone human to talk to; somebody whom she could actually touch and feel and not a Christ who died many years ago, a Christ who could only talk to her in the spirit. If only she could meet Waiyaki more often; if only he could stay near her, then Christ would have a bigger meaning for her. (p. 117)

Nyambura feels 'that the Christ who died could only be meaningful if Waiyaki was there for her to touch, for her to feel and talk to.' (p. 117) She knows that a Christ divorced from the relationships which are important to her in her life have no real meaning for her.

Amos Wilder and Paul Tillich both agree that a religion which is imposed upon a people from above as law, is not only meaningless, but also destructive. Ngugi shares the same belief. In the character of Joshua, Ngugi portrays the religious law given, the man who accepts without question the religion handed down to him by those he considers his superiors, the man who feels it his duty to impose the acceptance of the same religion on those under his control; and through the character of Nyambura, Ngugi condemns this imposed religious law as being destructive to the people it involves. Ngugi's development of Joshua as the religious law-giver who blindly accepts religion as it is handed down to him can be seen in the following four quotations:

Joshua was such a staunch man of God and such a firm believer in the Old Testament, that he would never refrain from punishing a sin, even if this meant beating his wife. He did not mind as long as he was executing God's justice. (pp. 35–36)

To him, Muthoni had ceased to exist on the very day that she had sold herself to the devil . . . The journey to the new Jerusalem with God was not easy. It was beset with temptation, but Joshua was determined to triumph, to walk with a brisk step, his eyes on the cross. Muthoni had been an outcast. Anything cursed here on earth would also be cursed in heaven. Let that be a warning to those who rebelled against their parents and the laws of God. (p. 62)

In fact he himself had always been puzzled by the fact that men of the Old Testament who used to walk with God and angels had more than one wife. But the man at the mission had said this was a sin, and so sin it had to be . . . (p. 113)

He prayed that the people should leave their ways and follow the ways of the white man. (p. 36)

Ngugi shows how this religion of Joshua's is met by the people it comes into contact with through his description of Joshua's wife, Miriamu:

60   However, one could still tell by her eyes that this was a religion learnt and accepted; inside the true Gikuyu woman was sleeping. (p. 39)

Through this description can be seen Ngugi's implied condemnation of the religion of Joshua. It was a religion which had to be *learnt* and *accepted* as it came down from an external source not a religion which grew and flourished from within. Ngugi's judgement of Joshua's brand of religion can be seen more directly through the thoughts of Nyambura.

> She cried. 'Waiyaki, you are mine, come back to me.' But he did not come. Her duty to her parents stood between him and her. A religion of love and forgiveness stood between them. No! It could never be a religion of love. Never, never. The religion of love was in the heart. The other was Joshua's own religion, which ran counter to her spirit and violated love. If the faith of Joshua and Livingstone came to separate, why, it was not good. If it came to stand between a father and his daughter so that her death did not move him, then it was inhuman. She wanted the other. The other that held together, the other that united. The voice that long ago said 'Come unto me all ye that labour and are heavy laden, and I will give you rest' soothed her and she wanted to hear it again and again . . . (pp. 154–55)

I feel it is interesting to note that Ngugi chooses to use the biblical words of Jesus – 'Come unto me all ye that labour and are heavy laden and I will give you rest' – in the context that he does, in the context of his condemnation of Joshua's strict law-like religion. It is of interest because Dr Paul Tillich uses the same bibilical passage to express the same condemnation. Speaking of these words of Christ, Tillich writes every adult is right in responding immediately to those words, as every adult is right in responding to them in all periods of his life and under all the conditions of his internal and external history. 'All ye that labour and are heavy laden . . .' these words, Tillich writes, are addressed to all men everywhere; they are universal and fit every human being and every human situation. Tillich explains what kind of burden it is that Jesus wishes to take from us:

> The burden He wants to take from us is the burden of religion. It is the yoke of the law; imposed upon the people of his time by the religious teachers. Those who labour and are heavy laden are those who are sighing under the yoke of religious law. (p. 101)

The religious law, Tillich continues, is the great attempt of man to overcome his anxiety and restlessness and despair, to close the gap within himself and to reach immortality, spirituality and perfection. **61**

The religious law demands that man accept ideas and dogmas; that he believe in doctrines and traditions, the acceptance of which is the condition of his salvation. And so man tries to accept them, even though they may have become strange or doubtful to him. James Ngugi has portrayed Joshua as a man in just such a predicament. Joshua feels that the religious laws of the white man must be strictly obeyed, even though some of them are a source of puzzlement to him, and must be so because they are the prerequisite for salvation, for entrance into the new Jerusalem. Dr Tillich goes on to say that the man caught within the religious law inevitably tries to impose it on other people, on his children or pupils. 'Many families are disrupted by painful tragedies and many minds are broken by this attitude of parents, teachers, and priests.' (p. 103). In the family of Joshua, Nyambura, Muthoni and Miriamu, Ngugi has presented a situation similar to that which Tillich describes. Here is a family broken, a family whose central unity has been lost because of the attempted imposition of an uncompromising religious law. In his development of Joshua and his family, Ngugi is commenting on the destructive and tragic nature of this kind of alien, external, and demanding religion.

In the course of his thesis, Amos Wilder devotes time to a discussion of the correct nature of the words of a religious message. He says that a religious message has real power only if the words it uses are alive. The words must be 'loaded'; they must carry a charge. 'They must strike down into the actual contemporary hungers and dreams of man.' (p. 95) Ngugi knows that this is true and expresses this thought by applying it to a real situation in his novel. Waiyaki stands before the people of Kameno, waiting to speak. Ngugi describes him through the people's eyes:

> Here again was the saviour, the one whose words touched the souls of the people. People listened and their hearts moved with the vibration of his voice. And he, like a shepherd speaking to his flock . . . (p. 110)

And what are the words which this saviour, this good shepherd who touches the heart and soul of the people, speaks. He does not speak of the Kingdom of God, of the new Jerusalem. He speaks of the school, of the tin roof which needs mending, of the desks, and pencils, and papers which the children have to have. Ngugi writes:

> He spoke on, pointing out the importance of learning; of acquiring all the wisdom that one could get. People wanted him to go on and on and on telling them the sweet words of wisdom. (p. 110)

Ngugi shows clearly how these words of Waiyaki are received by the people:

> When he sat down the people stood and, as if of one voice, shouted 'The Teacher! The Teacher! We want the Teacher . . . Our children must learn. Show us the way. We will follow.' (p. 110)

Waiyaki's, then, is a religious message, one which, Ngugi writes, touches the souls of the people, one which is directed not towards religious ideals but rather one which Waiyaki directs towards the concrete problems of his people in their actual situation. Proceeding further, Amos Wilder writes that if Jesus' word and deed searched and reconciled the hearts of those who heard him, it was not because he spoke general religious truths because he mediated an encounter with God at some timeless level. It was because in a fateful moment of his nation's destiny he invoked its supreme memories and loyalties. 'He exploited their relevant traditions by applying to the great prototypes of the past and to the potent images of the national destiny'. (p. 90) Again, James Ngugi brings across the thought expressed by these words of Amos Wilder in his novel, *The River Between*. Ngugi writes of Waiyaki:

> He turned to the people and in simple words reminded them of their history. 'It was before Agu and Agu, at the beginning of things that Murungu, the Creator, gave rise to Gikuyu and Mumbi . . .' He spoke of the great heroes of the tribe and mentioned Demi, Mathathi, Wachiori, Mugo wa Kibiro and Kamiri. He told them of the great victories that these heroes had over the Masai and other enemy tribes. It was because the hills were united that such great victories were possible.

Waiyaki then condemns those elements of the tribe which cry for vengeance against Joshua and his followers. He pushes for unity:

> That is what I have come to tell you today. We are all children of Mumbi and we must fight together in one political movement, or else we perish and the white man will always be on our back. Can a house divided against itself stand? (p. 171)

The people, again, are moved at these words and rise to shout, 'The Teacher! The Teacher!' Waiyaki has spoken to the people of their past, of heroes in their history, and of what needs to be done in the present for the future stability of their nation. And the people are clearly touched by these words. Ngugi knows that it is these kinds of words **63** which strike down into people's hearts and hold meaning for them. Ngugi has once more driven home his central point – religion must arise out of a people's total life situation; it must speak directly to those people within the context of their whole existence; within the context of their past history, their present experience, and their future destiny.

What James Ngugi develops in *The River Between*, then, is the theme that a people's religion and a people's way of life must be one; each must grow out of the other. Either one by itself is incomplete. *The River Between* is an image which I feel may justifiably be interpreted in the light of this theme. It represents the unity of the two separate forces. It is symbolic of the road between the two antagonistic forces which Waiyaki, Nyambura, and Muthoni attempted, each in their own way to travel, the road they knew was the only one which could give them a full and meaningful life. Honia River is described as flowing between the two opposing ridges, Makuyu and Kameno. On one side of the river the Christians of Makuyu conduct their Christmas celebrations; on the other side the tribe conducts its rite of circumcision. And it is here, on the banks of Honia, that Muthoni – a Christian from Makuyu – is made a woman of the tribe through circumcision, and here again that Waiyaki from Kameno and Nyambura from Makuyu come together in their embrace. Honia river is the site of these two symbolic acts of the coming together of the tribe and the Christian religion, and is itself, a symbol of that unity.

Ngugi's most striking clarification of Honia River as a symbol of tribal and Christian unity (and in broader terms of life and religion's unity) comes in the form of a biblical passage which Ngugi quotes through the thoughts of Nyambura. Nyambura has just denounced in her mind the harsh and sterile religion of Joshua, a religion which separates and causes pain. She relieves her frustration by reflecting upon the kind of religion which would be meaningful to her, a religion expressed simply and beautifully by the words of the Bible:

And she remembered: 'The wolf also shall dwell with the lamb, and the leopard shall lie down with the kid; and the calf and the young lions and the fatling together; and a little child shall lead them. And the cow and the bear shall feed; their young ones shall lie down together; and the lion shall eat straw like the ox. And the sucking child shall play on the hole of the asp, and the weaned child shall put his hand on the cockatrice's den. They shall not hurt nor destroy in all my holy mountain; for the earth shall be full of the knowledge of the Lord, as the waters cover the sea.' That was her religion. That was what she now wanted for her tribe. It was the faith that would give life and peace to all. (pp. 154–155)

This young Christian girl from Makuyu dreams of a future time of unity. And the dream centres on Waiyaki of the tribe from Kameno.

> So she clung to this now, as she prayed that Waiyaki would come back to her. (p. 155)

Waiyaki, too, has a similar vision, a vision which centres on Nyambura, and on the river:

> For a moment he dreamt the dream. It was a momentary vision that flashed across his mind and seemed to light the dark corners of his soul. It was a vision of a people who could trust one another, who would sit side by side singing the song of love which harmonised with music from the birds, and all their hearts would beat to the rhythm of the throbbing river. The children would play there, jumping from rock on to rock splashing the water which reached fathers and mothers sitting in the shade around talking, watching. Birds sang as they hovered from tree to tree, while farther out in the forest beasts of the land circled around . . . In the midst of all this Nyambura would stand. The children would come to her and she would talk to the elders. The birds too seemed to listen and even the beasts stopped moving and stood still. And a song arose stirring the hearts of all, and their longing for a new life in the future was reflected in the dark eyes of Nyambura. (p. 137)

And as Waiyaki and Nyambura stand mute together before the people under the ringing challenge of Kabonyi to deny each other, James Ngugi writes:

> And Honia River went on flowing through the valley of life, throbbing, murmuring an unknown song.

> *They shall not hurt nor destroy in all my holy mountains, for the earth shall be full of the knowledge of the Lord, as the waters cover the sea.* (p. 173)

NOTE

1. *The River Between.* All quotations in this article from Heinemann African Writers Series edition, first published London, 1965.

The Burnt-Out Marriage
and Burned-Up Reviewers

Jack B. Moore

The recent response of two frequent and influential critics of African
literature, England's Gerald Moore and Ghana's Ama Ata Aidoo, to Dr
Sarif Easmon's novel *The Burnt-Out Marriage* is both inadequate and
disappointing, because neither deals directly and specifically with the
book with much intensity, and because both reviewers appear instead
to criticise matters peripheral to the book itself, such as Dr Easmon's
supposed racism or his alleged tribalism or his imagined preference for
city (and therefore apparently Western) values over provincial, traditional ways.[1] Had Dr Easmon's novel been a racial or political or
sociological polemic, I could understand the extra-literary criticism,
though not the failure of either critic accurately to state what the
book's central concerns are. Or were the book sloppily written, the
failure of either critic to examine its literary values, its structure, descriptions, characterisations, motifs, would be excusable since few
critics like to waste space on inferior craftsmanship. Yet the phrase 'a
beautiful romantic fantasia' can be seen with a microscope embedded in
Miss Aidoo's review and 'considerable narrative skill' hidden in Moore's.

66 Both reviews are however overwhelmingly negative and conclude on curiously emotional notes for two such ordinarily expert critics: Miss Aidoo keens shrilly for the fate of African fiction and Moore gratuitously jibes at an African city that is not the locale of the novel and is never actually mentioned in the text.

Again, if the book were a total, good old-fashioned flop, one would not mind the reviews since bad books sometimes occasion bad criticism: who wants to bother writing well about some claptrap nonsense anyway; save the good stuff for when you're apt to be quoted. But Dr Easmon's novel is at the very least competent and I think it better than that. Its deficiencies are mostly minor, its major mistake so bad that, like the bum note the concert pianist sometimes hits, you tend to ignore it as atypical of its performer. Certainly when you compare the book to some of those chosen for publication in Heinemann's prestigious African Writers Series, you wonder why this particular work should be so viciously attacked. Books such as Kenneth Kaunda's *Zambia Shall Be Free*, which has all the force and insight of a YMCA tract on how to serve tea (a strange book for such a forceful and insightful man), or Cyprian Ekwensi's *People of the City*, which begins badly and then impossibly enough deteriorates, are incomparably worse yet have apparently achieved some status in the canon of African literature. Perhaps one reason for the puzzling antagonistic response, surely out of proportion even were the book bad, of these two critics, is that they still see themselves sallying to the African crusades swathed in the robes of 'Protector of the Culture', a justifiable function perhaps during the early, battling years of African literary criticism. Miss Aidoo sees Easmon as a frightening threat to African life, and even Moore, I sense, is not satisfied that Easmon sufficiently cherishes the old, traditional values. Perhaps after so many years of knocking down boorish foreigners and apologetic natives (Miss Aidoo is of course younger than Mr Moore, but she writes like a veteran), the critics have become battle fatigued, jittery at the flicker of what seems their common cultural-enemy's shadow. 'Boom boom' go the guns and another nasty neo-colonialist or westernised African is shot down. But I wonder if they know which ones are the enemy now?

I do not feel that either critic examines the book, what is really in the book, sufficiently. I also feel that both critics impose certain of their own predispositions upon the work without permitting the novel to declare its own forms and terms. I feel that this variety of unfocused or peripheral criticism is untrustworthy and especially dangerous to African literature where books are reviewed with relative infrequency and where, because of the volatile and burgeoning nature of African society, so many ideas, so many adherents and partisans of ideas **67** violently oppose each other. I feel that the texture of the work itself should be most important and therefore most diligently scrutinised by the critic, and not congeries of attitudes and experiences out of which the work may or may not arise. For this reason, I propose to examine both the reviews of Dr Easmon's novel and the book itself. My objective is not to attack either Miss Aidoo or Gerald Moore, for both have shown themselves excellent literary critics. My goal is to produce a more accurate reading of Easmon's book, which I take as a paradigm of any African book shuttled off-centre by misplaced critical force. I may, of course, be incorrect in my particular reading, but I do not think my method wrong; to stick as closely as possible to the text and ignore as much as I can those fuzzy, sometimes illusory shapes that hover in the background (or do they hang in the viewer's mind?) of any attempted work of art, like mirages about a target.

The ferocity of response from both reviewers indicates the impact Dr Easmon's novel made on them, though in each instance the critic seems acutely repelled by what appears on the surface a harmless enough book. Ordinarily so strong a response, positive or negative, means that the critic has been at least moved by the writer, that for some reason the writer's work has propelled itself beyond that pale, dull landscape most contemporary fiction drifts powerlessly into. But in each case the strong response has obscured the book Dr Easmon wrote and replaced it with one recreated in the critic's mind. Both critics, I am sure unconsciously, misrepresent the book.

Miss Aidoo, for example, hardly seems to be reviewing a novel at all when she examines *The Burnt-Out Marriage*. In its place she substitutes what is apparently a racist tract attacking black Africa and according to her 'creating havoc in people's lives'. Were the book truly accomplishing all this it would be a rare work indeed, and worthy of closer reading than Miss Aidoo has given it. She dismisses the work's novelistic pretensions by calling the plot 'a beautiful romantic fantasia'. This less than extensive aesthetic evaluation is then dropped for socio-political analysis: horror upon horrors, the book is neo-colonialist. In the essay itself Miss Aidoo is rather vaporous about exactly what constitutes neo-colonialism, and glides around precisely how and where it elsewhere displays itself. Never mind, she knows it exists and that Easmon's book is a by-product of it. 'The term "neo-colonialism(ist)",' she somewhat awkwardly writes, 'is after all not merely a figment of a paranoid politician's brain but an operative process: and ... this process, never mind how and where it manifests itself, is daily creating

68 havoc in people's lives. One may not be qualified enough to spot it in other fields, but certainly Dr Easmon's novel is plainly an artistic by-product of this brand of disorientation.' Frequently, neo-colonialism in Africa is discussed in economic terms. Dr Nkrumah for example wrote in *Consciencism* that he 'distinguished between two colonialism's, between a domestic one, and an external one. Capitalism at home is domestic colonialism.' For Miss Aidoo the term is largely racial, and it is (what she declares is) the book's racist attitude that most bothers her. 'There is an obvious racial complex about the narrative which generates a very uncomfortable feeling,' she writes. Then she quotes descriptions of four workers at the start of the book and claims that their 'ugliness' in each case 'has something to do with being black'. Now it is not unusual for black writers to accuse other black writers of exhibiting this variety of racism (and of course that white writers show it is practically axiomatic): James Baldwin charged Richard Wright with it, and Eldridge Cleaver in turn charged Baldwin. The implications of the accusation are particularly nasty and I think in each instance the evidence needs scrutiny. It is true, for example, that Easmon plunges the reader into his up-country world by introducing him to a number of racy characters who are black and who are generally described, at least facially, as grotesque. Is this racist?

I think that examination of the entire book reveals that it is filled with grotesque characters, but that these grotesques are perfectly suitable for the kind of novel Dr Easmon wrote. All these characters are black, but then so is everyone else in the book. Furthermore, a number of exceptionally handsome or beautiful characters operate throughout the text and these are also black. *The Burnt-Out Marriage* is a romance in the sense that Northrop Frye uses the term in *The Anatomy of Criticism*, or Richard Chase in *The American Novel and Its Tradition* (a book not solely about the American novel, incidentally), or in the sense Hawthorne used the term introducing most of his extended fictions. The romance is a looser form than the doggedly realistic novel, in that it tends to manipulate reality to the point of fantasy, and depicts its world through opposites: extremes of behaviour, good and evil, beauty and ugliness. The characters in a romance are usually quite limited (two-dimensional), but intense, in their emotions. They do not manifest a full range of emotions, but those responses they exhibit, along with the actions resulting from these emotions, are strong. They are passionate lovers and passionate haters. *Wuthering Heights* is an example of a romance, *Moby-Dick* is another, D. H. Lawrence's *The Plumed Serpent* a more recent model. *The Burnt-Out Marriage* is also a romance (though clearly not of the same quality as the others mentioned). It builds its world through displaying magic, the supernatural, through portraying **69** great beauty and ugliness, through passionate conflicts that literally consummate by fire. That the novel opens with some grotesque physical types fits into the pattern the book will follow.

The grotesques are black, but it is Miss Aidoo who sees black as a condition of their ugliness rather than as an adjective describing colour. Easmon is careful throughout to note colour disparity though he does not assign any moral condition or ideal of beauty to any one shade. In the opening chapter one face is described as 'odd, chocolate-coloured' and another is 'dark, ridiculous', but most fundamental grammar texts would explain that this means one face was odd *and* chocolate-coloured, and the other dark *and* ridiculous. Oddness is not an inherent condition of chocolate-coloured any more than ridiculous is an inherent condition of dark, except in Miss Aidoo's review. An unkind critic might ask why she assumes the link between colour and ugliness. Easmon himself carefully detaches physical beauty from moral behaviour. Each of the grotesques introduced at the book's outset, excepting Banky Vincent, will be sympathetically portrayed by the conclusion of the novel, just as several of the more attractive characters, Damba for instance, will be shown as morally corrupt. The homeliest male in the book and the most grotesque is also the blackest, and the most human and sympathetic. (The character is called 'White', ironically enough. Miss Aidoo, unless a printer's mistake has changed her meaning, erroneously states that he is the colour white.) Of another black and unattractive, native, the Rainmaker Gondomboh, Easmon writes that his 'personality . . . shone through his ugliness'. So there is an aesthetic reason for the grotesque characters, blackness does not seem to be the cause of their unattractiveness, and most of the grotesques are rather sympathetically treated.

The 'uncomfortable feeling' Easmon's alleged 'racial complex' gave Miss Aidoo might have been alleviated had she noted some of the other descriptions of the book's characters. Makallay, the novel's female protagonist, is radiantly beautiful and black, that is, African. Her specific colour is light brown, but surely Miss Aidoo is not the sort of racist who sees every shade away from true black that much further from perfection. Fernan Williams, who is a mulatto and apparently darker than Makallay, is described as being extremely attractive. Damba, a woman befriended by Makallay but who later betrays her, as a 'gorgeous nut-brown' complexion which does not prevent her from being eminently desirable. Francis Briwa, Makallay's husband, is quite dark, handsome, and intelligent, however questionable his behaviour might be sometimes (all the leading characters behave equivocally, even Makallay). Makallay's girlfriend and fellow wife to Briwa, Mahtah, is very dark. Her lips were 'of a natural purplish black', yet she too is beautiful. The black villagers are incidentally often described in attractive terms. I do not know therefore what would satisfy Miss Aidoo, unless all the black characters were black as black diamonds and beautiful and pure, and some blonde, blue-eyed whites were introduced up-country, as blotchy, spindly and decadent.

Miss Aidoo's other charges against the text seem similarly misdirected by her desire to read the book as a subversive attack against the unsullied integrity of Mother Africa. 'Except for the dubious Bankole Vincent,' she claims, 'everything Creole is good ... as compared to things native.' This both simplifies and distorts the text. The (part) Creole heroine, Makallay, is certainly not all or even basically good, just as the conventional villain, her (non-Creole) husband Francis, is not all or even basically evil. One of the book's central ironies is the admixture of vice, folly, and good in the major characters, who on the surface seem to be extremes of innocence and evil. Mr Gerald Moore makes a similar misreading here based upon a prejudgement connected to Miss Aidoo's, and I shall discuss the matter further when I come to the English critic's argument. Here I shall simply point out that one Creole, Fernan Williams, is anything but good. She is clever and attractive, but also snide to nearly everyone including her supposed friend Makallay. She sleeps with a man she hates for half a year, after running away from her husband, and then steals the hated lover's money. In so doing she gives him more dignity than he possesses at any other time in the book, making her even less sympathetic. She leaves town letting her mother remain behind and vulnerable in the village. Another Creole mentioned in the text, Banky Vincent's sister, 'the unspeakable bitch that she is', Makallay says, 'was caught red-handed in adultery' just six weeks after her marriage. Half-Creole Makallay is caught after two years. She stays six months in the centre of Creoledom and returns home pregnant. There is nothing particularly romantic about this and the fact hardly adds lustre to the Creole city as a 'good' place. The book is primarily about a provincial town peopled by provincial characters, and Creoledom is off-centre, peripheral to it. But clearly the concept of regional or tribal values sketched in the text is ambivalent and reveals little bias on Easmon's part. True, the villagers, the non-Creoles, have definite and suspicious attitudes towards Creoledom, but Dr Easmon surely cannot be blamed for reporting what, more than likely, would historically have been thought about the Creoles in his fictional up-country chiefdom.

Elsewhere Miss Aidoo, like countless African and English and American (and Lithuanian, I suppose, and Bosnia-Herzogovinian) critics **71** before her, condemns the author for reporting his view of reality rather than some ideal the critic in nationalistic ardour has dreamed. Usually the critic claims historical accuracy. The gambit in this instance could be called 'I know more about Africa than you do,' and many critics these days play it. 'My ideal Africa is the real one' could be its sub-title. 'Somehow one feels like telling Dr Easmon,' the professorial Miss Aidoo hectors, 'that the first wife of any West African Chief ... would be anything but untidy or in any way lacking in dignity. But it is obvious,' she sighs, 'that the author knows nothing about West Africa.' Well, I do not know anything about Miss Aidoo, but I do know that Dr Easmon is an African, has lived in West Africa most of his life, that the Prime Minister of his country thinks him learned enough to appoint him frequently to bodies directly concerned with affairs of state, that Dr Easmon lived a good part of his youth in exactly the sort of town he describes in his novel, near the Guinean border. All this may have nothing to do with his book, but that is one way to counter the gambit when critic challenges author to 'I know more about Africa.' Another ploy is to stay away from the book and ask other Africans if they've seen sloppy first wives in out-of-the-way chiefdoms and they generally laugh and say yes, and of course if you travel a bit you see them yourself. But the sport is pretty senseless because it takes you away from the book. If you read the book, first of all you see that the chief's first wife though sometimes sloppy is one of the most dignified and regal characters in the text, that the first wife grows in moral stature as the plot develops, that she becomes a kind of sad, noble symbol of the old way of life, dusty maybe but still grand. And maybe you are stupid and do not know as much about Africa as Miss Aidoo does, but maybe you remember vaguely Queen Victoria, who was pretty dowdy and rarely on anyone's best-dressed list, no Twiggy she, yet she had a queenliness to her that few disputed, and so you say wives of African chiefs are probably the same sometimes, they grow old, a bit fat, sloppy, they sag too, *sic transit gloria gluteus maximus.*

Most of Miss Aidoo's remaining criticisms attack the book, or Easmon, as anti-African. She does not so much condemn the novel as novel, but the author as Western. That this is true seems to me dubious and, more important, aesthetically irrelevant. Easmon's background is both African and cosmopolitan and he naturally writes from his background. Beyond his specifically African upbringing, he has the same broadly classical education that most modern intellectuals share, the same education shared by Miss Aidoo, I would guess. 'The author betrays,' Miss Aidoo writes, 'his conscious Western scholarship by letting old man Brassfoot translate a whole chunk from the Greek Xenophon.' Why Miss Aidoo employs the word 'betrays' I am not sure, since Dr Easmon's education would naturally have been part Western. I do not believe he has ever tried to conceal this fact. More to the point, his character Bob Brassfoot has received a part Western education, and quite naturally as a sort of intellectual feat he recites part of a particularly beautiful Western classic he has once studied. This is a schoolboy trick and Dr Easmon uses it cleverly in a number of ways. I believe a critic would function better in trying to see how the little interlude fits into the book than in carping about the Western subject matter extrapolated into African education. It may be that Brassfoot would have been better prepared to work in his store had he learned accounting, say, rather than Greek classics. Perhaps a study of D. A. Fagunwa rendered in the original would have offered him a greater sense of African literary greatness. But this would falsify his history. Bob Brassfoot did not learn about Zimbabwe or about Chaka the Great and Dr Easmon cannot pretend that he did. So he includes the kind of remembrance Bob Brassfoot might have shown off with. The passage and its commentary also make Brassfoot seem more real to us and more sympathetic. For a time he is part of the world of Luluahun but mostly he is peripheral to it: the quotation reveals this. He is kindly, educated, essentially helpless because of his inferior position and because he is outside the social system of the village that Briwa rules. He is one of the many characters who will be unable to affect the fate of either the two principals in their developing struggle. The Xenophon underscores his difference, his isolation. And precisely because he is associated with such an ancient quotation so arcane to the immediacy of the village life, he is seen as powerless to disturb the relentless conclusion of the book, just as nearly everyone is. Moreover his discussion of Xenophon reflects several of the book's themes. 'The things that raise life to meaningfulness have nothing to do with riches and social position,' he says. 'All life is more or less a tribulation . . . why struggle to have?' His words are wise but banal after his eloquent recital: still they do comment on Francis Briwa's fate. Briwa bargains away his sexual potency so precious to any man but achingly so to the African chief, in order to obtain his Paramount Chieftancy, power, position. His life at its zenith becomes a handful of dust.

So the brief, relatively unimportant interlude operates successfully in a number of ways. I suppose old man Brassfoot might have quoted some apt African proverbs: there are several placed throughout the text, wherever they fit. But then that would have been untrue to his character and to his time. Yes, Xenophon seems a bit foreign to the small provincial village and Easmon knows it. He immediately precedes **73** the section by describing the parade of a devil rustling in raffia and topped with a black mask, jiggling down the street. Xenophon and the devil clash as Western and African so frequently clash (and merge) in Africa. But Miss Aidoo's automatic response to anything Western has prevented her from seeing how right, in a small way, the passage with Brassfoot is.

Finally, Miss Aidoo objects to the book's politics, claiming in a nearly apocalyptic vision that it is destructive to Africa, her Africa. 'Of course politically the book is a total disaster' she announces. 'We have all been crying for works of *committed* African genius. *The Burnt-Out Marriage* is worse than uncommitted. It fans already smouldering fires of regional dissensions and petty ethnic complexes.' I hope I have already shown that the book's ethnic content is ambivalent. No clear picture of clan superiority emerges: good and evil, intelligence and ignorance transcend tribal affiliation. The book does show how one tribe stereotypes another, how regional dissensions colour personal relationships. These are not central issues in the book, they are mingled with a number of themes: primarily the book is about individuals and not about sociological abstractions. The stereotyping and tribal distrust it shows are, I think even Miss Aidoo would admit, part of the African picture, and Easmon would only betray his art or radically distort it were he not to include this slice of provincial life. Would the book have escaped political disaster (of course) had Easmon falsified reality? Would the book have escaped total political disaster (of course) had Easmon ignored the truth? What concept of political success is Miss Aidoo advocating? What sort of commitment does she require of writers if not to the truth as they see it?

Perhaps it is time for critics to stop demanding a particular variety of commitment from writers beyond the commitment to show the world as they see it, and to show that world with artistic vitality and rightness. Novelists are not members of parliament. They have no obligation to improve mankind, only to show mankind to itself. They should not be required to portray a morally grand universe or a morally ideal nation. They may be evil. Their books may be pernicious to the public good, or some may think them so. But the novelist need not leap to the whip of the demanding critic who sees himself as policeman, philanthropist, nun, priest, or doctor to the world. The novelist goes his own way and the critic must, at first, follow. He must see precisely what the novelist is doing, and how well. Then if he sees the novelist's work accurately, he may go beyond strictly literary evaluation and decide exactly what the politics and philosophy of a book are, and how

useful they are to the public good. But the critic must deal accurately with the book's content first. And if he narrowly demands that the writer follow some formula or other, that the writer uphold some nationalistic or even racial cause or other, the critic is bound to see mostly his own residual limitations in a book, his own prejudices reflected and blinding him, and not the author's work as it exists in its own integrity, or lack of integrity. Were fires of regional dissension smouldering in Africa, Easmon would be within his rights to report it.

But the critic's first function is not to judge the social benefit or disaster a book can bring, this is always tenuous anyway, and depends so much upon what the individual critic thinks beneficial or harmful, but to analyse and evaluate exactly what the writer has done. In accomplishing this difficult task, I am not sure that the critic gains from starting out with lorryloads of sociological preconditions, political slogans, and artistic blindfolds.

Gerald Moore's review of *The Burnt-Out Marriage* is less spirited than Miss Aidoo's, more seemingly objective in its language, until its conclusion, more urbane, even world-weary in its approach to the novel. Moore writes the way a man speaks who is trying to smother a yawn: phrases drone along with lovely somnolence: 'what we see is a co-existence and dynamic interaction of values and attitudes which are often as mingled in the individual as they are in the social context,' where 'social context' for example is somnolese for 'society', but his distaste for the book becomes quite obvious as his prose lumbers on to its conclusion, where he becomes surprisingly sarcastic about two characters from the book, as though they had annoyed him the way real girls might. 'Without regret,' he sums up, holding the novel gingerly at arm's length with his fingertips before sleepily dropping it in the wastebasket, 'the reader watches the final departure of these tiresome girls for the sophisticated delights of Freetown, whose society is infinitely more derivative and insecure than the one so easily disposed of here.' The remark is doubly surprising because Freetown has actually very little relevance to Dr Easmon's book, and its alleged derivativeness and insecurity utterly inapposite as a critical topic. This puzzling outburst suggests that Moore's glutinous prose smooths over an attitude toward the book as harsh as Miss Aidoo's. Certainly some of his literary objections appear shaky, as though he were, unconsciously I am sure, trying to discover rational arguments to back up a subjective, extra-literary response. For example he writes that the novel 'displays considerable narrative skill, but it . . . suffers from a certain diagrammatic inevitability of plot.' In an almost totally negative review it is strange to see an aside tucked in about narrative skill, for ordinarily narrative skill is precisely what the good **75** novelist seeks. If you find it in a book ordinarily then you consider the book a literary success. Narrative skill is what the art of the novel is about, yet even though Easmon has the talent to a considerable degree, it does not help him much. The glancing praise is immediately swept away. The work 'suffers from a certain diagrammatic inevitability of plot', Moore writes. But how is that a flaw? *Oedipus Rex* has inevitability of plot. So has *Hamlet*. So has *Things Fall Apart*. All concern inevitably doomed protagonists. So does *The Burnt-Out Marriage*. The book may be bad: it is clearly not as fine an African novel as Achebe's. But its inevitability is beside the point, or rather necessarily part of its plot structure. Perhaps Moore attaches some cabalistic significance to his word 'diagrammatic' that clarifies his meaning. I read it as padding for inevitability, the sound of two thunderbolts rolling from the temple instead of one, two pebbles plopping in the pond.

Mr Moore's antipathy to the book is clear throughout his review. Easmon's work is old-fashioned, he says, because Easmon writes of a man destroyed through ignorance of a system beyond his own traditional one. Easmon is unaware that this 'well-trodden ground offers little to challenge the expectations of the reader.' Moore is apparently the reader and we will all admit he has read far more African novels than Easmon. Still, Moore graciously provides an out for Easmon if he ever has the temerity to publish another book – perhaps the review was, in fact, intended as a *caveat* for aspiring African novelists: greetings from the oracle. Easmon can write this kind of old-fashioned book if his imagination is outside both systems – the old and the new, the traditional and the apparently un-traditional. Moore stands solemnly by his gates barring the old-fashioned and the subjective, but one suspects slightly to the left and right of his gorgonian stare novelists will slip through unopposed, as they always have. To say a motif is old-fashioned is to say in fact that it is traditional. The novel of conflicting cultures that Scott wrote, that Henry James wrote, that Fenimore Cooper wrote, that William Faulkner and D. H. Lawrence wrote and that Saul Bellow writes, I use Western writers purposefully here, is invariably tempered by subjectivity to some degree, and some of the best novels in this tradition are almost totally subjective. Moore qualifies his pronouncement by stating the shaping imagination need only stand 'to some extent outside both systems,' but this is exactly where Easmon stands. Moore admits that Easmon presents the representative of the old society, Chief Briwa, 'with sympathy and even compassion'. But, Moore writes, 'the sympathy is guarded by a visable conviction that Briwa is simply on the wrong side, and that [his] personal qualities cannot mitigate this fact.' If by wrong side Moore means losing side, I do not understand how Moore can blame Easmon with presenting historic fact. Sad but true, generally the new replaces the old. Urban replaces rural. Third wives will become secretaries and eventually give way to computers, I suppose. We may lament the loss, but will be programmed to love the computers. Even now in Africa population control councils advise us that photostatic reproduction is the safest variety. Moore speaks of the dynamic interaction of values within the individual that marks the African personality as though one could select those items of one's culture which are most pleasing and match them with others of equal benefit for some intersecting culture. Here one retains multiple subservient wives, there one plucks an architectural advance or two and readjusts the judicial system to make it fairer to women. This is what Briwa attempts. But it does not work, in fiction or in reality, and this is what Easmon shows. The dynamic process is sometimes destructive and frequently if not always uncontrollable. When you electrify a village, you cannot really direct its cultural flow.

Similarly, the critic should avoid diverting the flow of a novel's energy into self-fabricated literary or sociological channels. What Easmon does well, his narrative skill for example, Moore barely notices. But he wants Easmon to write according to Moore's concept of the 'modern' African novel and of Africa as well. Moore does not approve, I would guess, that Chief Francis Briwa is thwarted, defeated by such a silly woman as Makallay. But that is precisely the nature of the cultural change Easmon chronicles. Francis does not get what he wants and Makallay does, and what is dignified and strong in his way of life is destroyed partly by what is foolish and shallow in Makallay, who endures: but Easmon is not culpable. History's unpleasant lesson is that when two cultures clash, shoddier elements sometimes emerge to last. Time erodes febrile, antiquated traditions and grand ones alike. When two individuals from different societies oppose each other, personal greatness and integrity do not invariably triumph. Nor is Makallay even a symbol for modernity or the urban society or Westernised, romanticised Africa. Like the schoolteacher in Soyinka's *The Lion and the Jewel*, she has collected only a few tinselled surface pieces of the supposedly democratic, advanced, brave new world.

Moore also objects that Easmon seems to share Makallay's attitude towards traditional provincial life. He is irritated with Makallay's 'assumptions of her innate superiority to the 'natives' as a Moslem and a Freetown-reared Susu, [and] it soon becomes clear that he [Easmon] shares these assumptions and has built his plot around them.' Thus the supposedly progressive Paramount Chief of the Sowannah, Francis Briwa, is doomed to extinction simply by being what he is, a **77** polygamist and, of course, a secret pagan.' Thus, Moore criticises what he assumes are Easmon's assumptions about the Chief, about Makallay, and about provincial and Freetown life – if the 'Luawa' of the book can indeed be equated with Freetown, a questionable critical device. Now an author's assumptions are not always easy to discover because they filter through the distorting lens of his book. Even when an author speaks in what is seemingly his own voice, as Thackeray does in *Vanity Fair*, you cannot trust the authorial voice to be identical to the real Thackeray's, for it is rather the printed voice of Thackeray appearing publicly in the book. I hope I am not belabouring the point, but I think it is important because both Miss Aidoo and Gerald Moore criticise *The Burnt-Out Marriage* not only because it does not conform to their pre-conditions for the African novel, but because they do not like what they assume are its author's assumptions towards his characters and towards Africa.

I would say next that an author's assumptions, his world view, are his own business, that what he does with them in the book is more to the point. The artistic use made of what are perhaps authorial convictions should be the central critical concern. Let me admit for argument's sake what I do not believe, and what analysis of the book will not support, that Easmon is a racist, that he is contemptuous of up-country life and entirely enthralled by the Freetowns of Africa. What of it? The critic should attend first of all to how well the artist puts his novel together, how strong are his characterisations. The work of art first, then perhaps the underlying ideas. Anyway, it should be obvious that a first-class work of art can be constructed from the most odious ideas. How many today would subscribe to the more appalling elements of Dante's Catholicism, or Milton's Puritanism? What the writer shows and how well he shows it is what needs analysis and criticism. Never mind what Moore or Miss Aidoo think are Easmon's attitudes towards his chief characters and their predicament; how does Easmon show them in action, what information does he supply about them? What the writer intends is less important than what he does. So what are the facts about Chief Briwa and Makallay? Trust the tale, not the teller, D. H. Lawrence said. What does the tale of *The Burnt-Out Marriage* tell us?

The book tells us Chief Briwa is 'fundamentally . . . a good man. But he was born into times and circumstances that doomed him almost always to show up in a bad light.' He is strong, resourceful, intelligent, willing and sometimes eager to modify the ways of his village to take advantage of what he considers the benefits of modern, non-village society.

'Francis was no longer a "pure" Sowannah Chief . . . Western influences had made an impact on him.' He has instituted 'new, humane' changes in his native court, and has constructed housing for his people that contains 'something both native, and, at the same time, revolutionary in Africa.' He is not radical, but a liberal-conservative. He chips and patches the old way – or as Gerald Moore calls it, the traditional way, though urban or Western society is traditional too – never really dismantling any essential part of his village structure, never basically modernising it either. Unlike Achebe's Okonkwo, he does not try to stop time, unlike – some neo-colonialists might say – Ghana's Nkrumah, he does not try to move time forward too rapidly. He is like a man stepping from temporarily safe ground part way into a rapidly moving current. Because he is strong he goes out farther than most. And because new currents are sometimes treacherous and because they cannot be controlled, he is destroyed, maybe faster than he would have been had he remained on shore or even plunged quickly far out. I do not suppose Easmon means that invariably the half-way man is destroyed, but he does convincingly portray the destruction of this strong but never fully determined provincial ruler. In a way, Briwa's attitude towards Makallay represents his attitude towards the new ways. He is deeply attracted to her but never really understands her. He feels that despite her obviously different upbringing she will fit harmoniously into her position in the village and in his compound. His ignorance of her unsuitability to become a part of provincial society contributes heavily to his vulnerability and finally to his destruction.

At first, Briwa seems innocent of his own downfall. His motives in changing village life slightly are honest, he has no wish to make Makallay unhappy, and nothing in his education would indicate to him that their union might prove unsatisfactory to her. After all, he is the chief and it would be an honour to be selected as his bride. But in falling back upon the tradition of the chief, even while chipping at the clay edges of traditional village life, Briwa's culpability is exposed in at least two ways. I mention these ways because Moore, it seems to me, presents Briwa as a sort of pleasant puppet dangling motiveless from the sophisticated, half-Western fingertips of Dr Easmon. First, Briwa wants the best of two worlds, the new and the old, the provincial and the urban. He wants sanitary housing and his pick of wives; a fairer legal system and absolute dominance at home. But cultures are not like ticky-tacky houses. You cannot select just those factory-built picture windows you want installed in the hut without creating other changes in the activities within. In his own situation, he cannot modify the lives of others without disturbing his own. Secondly, even as traditional chief, a role whose **79** obligations he actively seeks, Briwa is something of a failure. He is sterile and can give none of his wives children. What would be worse to the partly emancipated woman, he cannot give two of his wives sexual satisfaction, and we do not know about the others. Village society all over Africa supposedly believes strongly in the traditional proverb 'there is no wealth where there are no children', and in Briwa's compound there is no wealth. Satiric jesters sing of this deficiency: 'Chief Briwa beds with many a girl, But what does he all through the night?' So the wives can only feel maternally or sexually unsatisfied. Briwa had himself as a younger man helped his ageing father by sleeping with one of the older man's wives, apparently as an act of simple charity, to keep cuckoldry in the family. But he unfortunately has no sons to perform a similar service for him. The point is that he accepts the special privileges of the chief but is unable to fulfil the special obligations. While he will import some Western ideas, including a more equitable court, he will not subscribe to ideas of sexual equality within his home. Insensitivity to his double standard helps destroy him.

Briwa's fall may be destined by forces beyond his control, but his movement towards the destructive flame is partly self-directed. As a young man he bargained with a powerful medicine man to receive the chieftaincy he was not favoured for. The terms of his victory, the price, included his future childlessness. Another medicine man, Gondomboh the Rainmaker, predicts that should his wife become pregnant, his life will end in flames. Of course he cannot reforge his destiny. He remains childless and burns to death shortly after he learns his favourite wife has been impregnated by another man. But he is not simply an innocent victim of supernatural fury. He has pursued his fate all along. His passion to become chief by any means, even if it demands his sterility and thus subverts his role as husband and chief, reveals his headlong chase after destruction. His passion for Makallay that for so long blinds him to what his wife has become and then possesses him with murderous hate, enflames him long before the hot, real fire from a household oil lamp splashes his body. Like innumerable heroes of Greek and African myth, he enmeshes himself in his fate, seems to follow it wilfully, so that when he is trapped we can both assert the mystery of a universe that suddenly trips the essentially good man headlong to his death, and see once again how man helps build the trick that eventually destroys him.

Makallay, in one line of reasoning the instrument of Briwa's disintegration, is dramatically much less interesting than he, but equally ambivalent. Both Gerald Moore and Miss Aidoo see her in the book as

the sophisticated, chic, beautiful, Creole-Susu, Freetown exemplar of what Moore calls 'Western individualist romanticism'. They also imply that this is her role in Easmon's mind. Moore points out her arrogance and suggests that Easmon agrees with her claims to superiority. I myself am not certain of Dr Easmon's intentions here, nor do they particularly concern me. What is important however is the way Makallay reveals herself to us within the frame of the book: again, trust the tale and not the teller. First, she is beautiful, second she is an outsider not conditioned to village ways, and what sympathy she gains results from this position. She is the kind of woman whose beauty and grace endow her with far more power, because of her effect on men, than she has the wisdom to use intelligently. It would be strange if the otherwise cynical Dr Easmon should establish this variety of the species as his ideal. In the book, as a person she is pretty much of a flop, and hardly seems fit symbol of Creole-Susu or urban supremacy.

Her first act is a total failure. She pays the fine for a Sowannah wife so that the woman may leave her apparently cruel husband. In itself a charitable act, Makallay's impetuous behaviour causes unspoken criticism of her husband since it is made possible by his new legal system and since it is contrary to Sowannah tradition. Commendable humanity turns into foolish meddling when Makallay wheedles Briwa into placing the woman, Damba, in one of his new houses. Everyone knows Damba is incapable of repaying kindness with kindness, for her sympathetic affections have become burnt-out too. Eventually Damba steals a gold ear-ring from Makallay. And after confronting Damba with her knowledge of the theft, Makallay gives her the other ear-ring too. Another character justly sees this act as 'reckless'. Damba later allies herself with Makallay's greatest enemy in the chief's compound, his first wife, and ultimately spies on Makallay. To round out her distinguished service, Damba beds with Briwa, disgracing both Makallay and the chief. 'Yet,' one wife thinks, 'he could lay aside all his dignity as Paramount Chief to sneak in broad daylight into the bed of a bitch and slave like Damba! What would the Chiefdom say if they knew their chief had elected to consort with the reject of an unknown farmer, an anonymous reject one of his own wives had bought out of charity?' So much for Makallay as welfare worker and judge of character.

During the second half of the book especially, when she is pregnant following her adulterous affair with a Luawa (Freetown?) Creole, Makallay increasingly lies and cheats to prevent Francis from knowing the truth. None of her lies is particularly clever and none ennobles her character. Lie only leads to lie, accusation to counter-accusation, as Makallay tries to rebut the claims made against her by Briwa's first, and extremely loyal wife, Mah Mahtoe. The conflict between the two wives **81** is maintained on a decidedly unromantic level. Mahtoe by chance notices Makallay naked in the bathroom and observes the changes pregnancy has caused in Makallay's nipples. She tells Briwa and Briwa charges Makallay, whose response is to label the honest old woman a liar: 'You expect this old witch to tell the truth about me?' Mahtoe is innocent of lying and Makallay knows it, and only reveals her own hypocrisy in accusing the, to her, sloppy but dignified woman.

Since in this book we do not see Makallay's lover until the fiery denouement, and then only briefly, we can only judge him through her.[2] Since she describes him in the most conventional terms, therefore revealing her shallowness, he seems anything but a worthy adversary for Briwa. Therefore their affair lacks glamour or romantic appeal. Further, one or both have bungled to the extent that Makallay is pregnant. Little about the interlude supports Makallay as a romantic ideal. In fact, Easmon insures otherwise. When Briwa wants to sleep with her on her return from Luawa, Makallay's excuse is that she has her menstrual period and so cannot. I doubt that Guinevere was so clinical with King Arthur. Surely this is a strange way to create a symbol of 'Western individualist romanticism'. Now Mah Mahtoe does increase in nobility as the book progresses, as Makallay does not. Miss Aidoo noted Mahtoe's sloppiness but missed her dignity. Throughout the book Mahtoe, though childless, tries to understand Briwa and attempts to keep their relationship the old, traditional one between Chief and wife. 'She loved him now, as she had loved him when he was young, with all the emotion and fidelity of heart of which she was capable. Anything that touched his honour she felt more deeply than he did himself.' Not implicated in his self-destruction, she attempts to stay his unhappy decline. Unfavoured in bed, in time of crisis she 'took charge completely, efficiently, devotedly of his affairs; no matter whether there was anything of importance on hand Mahtoe, never mind her being ungainly and unattractive, gave him the assurance he needed.' Mahtoe keeps the old rhythms, the seasonal changes and harmonies, as Makallay does not. She gives strength to Francis and does not undermine or destroy him, holds 'him securely as a cable tethering him to sanity'. And she has a beauty too, not flashy but deep, as 'dressed in a silk taimlay and a lappa as gorgeously worked as her husband's', she bursts through a band of women and dances laughing into Francis' arms to celebrate the harvest. 'Her arms swayed with hypnotic snakelike sinuosity; her hips melted into rhythm; her feet and the music's beat were as wedded as were the drummer's fingers to his drum.' She scores heavily confronting Makallay: 'What a pity you did not send me, too,' she tells Francis in front of
the younger wife, 'up to Luawa years back! I, too, could have come

back with a beautiful ring round my finger and carrying a bastard child to wear like a chain of disgrace round your neck.' She throws herself on the floor out of despair and Francis demands she control herself. She rises dusty but 'immensely dignified and tragic', and walks from the room, 'heavy as a figure of doom'. And all that Makallay has now, at this moment, is 'enmity' towards her, without dignity or grace. Makallay's hypocrisy, her superficiality, her unfaithfulness – these are feeble defences to balance Mahtoe's simple integrity in upholding her husband's lost cause.

I do not want to imply that Makallay is an unalloyed villainess, for this would create a perversion of the text. I do want to point out that she is never much more than an extraordinarily attractive woman with pleasing ways who makes mistake after mistake. She is even incapable of sending a note to her lover without causing great turmoil. She sinks beyond her depth in cutting away from her role as traditional wife. Yet in a way her responses are no more her fault that Francis' are his. For the first time in her life she is in love, as she has apparently been allowed to conceive of love in her urban African society, tainted if you will with Western ideas. She is for the first time enthralled, aroused, awakened. She has not the strength of character to deny this love and she succumbs to it. Neither can she break cleanly with Francis, even if her society would permit a clean break. But Easmon rarely glorifies her acts, though he does show how Francis becomes progressively brutalised as selfish passions eat away his once more sympathetic character. For example, during the final confrontation between the two, Francis tries to beat Makallay for her transgressions. As chief or as dishonoured husband this is his right. Even beyond the African traditions validating his anger are certain vaguely universal patterns. Surely if ever a man had cause to beat his wife he does, for she has lied to him, cheated on him, made him a fool, slept in another man's bed. His desire to strike back is understandable. But then he says that perhaps his blows will root out the unborn foetus from Makallay. From exhibiting the excusable state of anger Father Tempel called in his classic *Bantu Philosophy* 'the evil will excited or provoked', Briwa passes to 'the pervert or destroyer' who annihilates being. At the same time, we cannot forget that Makallay has provoked him to this condition. And never for long can we forget her other weaknesses or deficiencies. Trying to post a simple note, this supposedly urban-cultured woman reveals that she cannot write. Even her beauty becomes on occasion grotesque. Just as the village doctor 'was trying to erase from his mind that he was looking at probably the most beautiful breasts he would see in his life', Makallay hacks her phthisic cough and spits blood on his shirt. From the interesting if troublesome **83** woman she appears at the book's start, Makallay seems quite trivial beside Francis and Mah Mahtoe and even the tortured Banky Vincent at the book's conclusion. As Francis' body burns and his other wives led by Mah Mahtoe wail their loss, the girl Mahtah introduces herself as 'one of the chief's wives' and Makallay primly corrects her as (Briwa smoulders upstairs): 'You were, Mahtah . . . As Gondomboh predicted, Francis has died by fire.'

So criticism of the text on the grounds that it is pro-Creole or anti-provincial or racist or that its author worships its main female character seems dubious. Miss Aidoo ended her critique with the exclamation 'May the good Lord help Africa!' if Easmon's book is typical of the new literature, yet her lament is not borne out by the book. Gerald Moore wearily waves the two 'tiresome girls' off to Freetown, which he seems to think is fit punishment for them. Moore appears determined to protect from any taint of attack the provincial life that he feels Francis represents and Easmon dislikes. I do not think that African village life will be saved by condemning *The Burnt-Out Marriage*. Undoubtedly there was a time when critics needed to be wary of anything faintly smacking of racism in African literature, when sociologists needed extra-sharp eyes to ferret out stereotyped anti-traditional Africa propaganda. But the vestiges of this traditional response seem old-fashioned when so wrongfully applied to Easmon's book.

Here this kind of criticism seems to set up the limitations of a book in much the same way that Hollywood constructs war-time streets to be destroyed. You construct a shaky front and knock it down, and unless the audience travels behind the façade they never notice that the creation is false, without foundations. That is what Miss Aidoo and Gerald Moore appear, unconsciously, to have done. They have abstracted from Easmon's book a set of conflicts and attitudes that do not in fact seem to exist in the fabric of the work itself. They have not examined the book, but what they assume are the assumptions behind the book. They consider the book a failure because it does not conform to certain standards that simply do not seem germane to Easmon's work. In doing this they fail to report on the book's true strengths and weaknesses. Neither notices the ambivalence in Makallay's character. Neither sees the details fashioning Briwa's fall. Neither reports on the interesting growth of Mah Mahtoe as a foil for Makallay. Neither begins to analyse the interesting treatment of sex in the book, and sex is not one of the major successes of African fiction.

Moore mentions the 'discreetly' lesbianic relationship between Mak-**84** allay and the darkly beautiful, young Mahtah, but drops the issue.

There is in fact nothing discreet about the sexual passion the two show for each other, and the matter fits neatly into the pattern of Easmon's frank though muted revelation of the village sex life. There is also, for example, some interesting and to me honest sounding talk between wives concerning which wife sleeps with Francis. Probably because of his guilt feelings over the price and method of attaining the chieftancy, and through rational fears of being unable to father a child, Francis is not a good lover. He seems incapable of lighting a spark in anyone save the treacherous Damba, who feeds his ego by achieving almost instant orgasm with him – or with anyone else, for that matter. Damba is also of distinctly inferior status, thus decreasing any latent fears of inadequacy Francis might possess through his failure with the 'superior' Makallay. At any rate he cannot satisfy either Makallay or Mahtah, his youngest wives, and in the absence of a suitable male lover – also of course not wanting to break customary law – they clearly maintain a homosexual relationship.[3] Homosexuality, so the myth goes, is unknown to Africa except where introduced by perverse whites. But it is in fact, rather common, as a recent article in *Presence Africaine* shows. Scattered references throughout *The Burnt-Out Marriage* indicate the intensity of feeling between Makallay and Mahtah. When Makallay befriends Damba, Mahtah is obviously jealous, just as she is jealous of Makallay's close friend Fernan Williams. Throughout the book Makallay and Mahtah admire each other's bodies in a particularly personal fashion. 'Makallay . . . looked up so intently into Mahtah's face that she made her have all the discomfort of a blush. "How beautiful you are, little one!" Makallay murmured.' A few moments later Makallay, in bed, tells Mahtah of her male lover and pulls her down close. 'For a whole minute Mahtah lay on her chest, both of them trembling in little spasms.' Following this climactic revelation, Mahtah displays no jealousy: this she apparently reserves for other women. Makallay then shows Mahtah proof of her pregnancy, the change in her breasts, which Mahtah cups and shakes 'gently up and down'. Then Mahtah hugs and kisses her friend 'with the passion of a lover'. The intertwined sexual relationships between Francis and Damba and his wives is not prominently stressed in the text but it is clearly, honestly and not too sensationally reported.

Easmon also describes large numbers of people and communal movements successfully. The scenes connected with sowing time – the rituals, dances, the visit to the Rainmaker, the satiric songs – are all interestingly depicted yet never seem included for mere local colour. They are integrated into the body of the novel, wisely adding spice to the story and evoking the milieu of the characters involved in the **85** narration. Similarly well handled is the section telling of Fernan William's dishonest but crafty theft of Banky Vincent's cash. Fernan's mother sagely comments 'for six months she was sleeping with Mr. Vincent. She did not even like him . . . I wonder if any amount of money can ever compensate a woman for six months of *that*.' Banky's response to the theft is stunned and then wild. Easmon combines in the interlude strong characterisation, native detail, a sense of comedy merging with the pathetic, that reveals him a writer capable of achieving varied effects smoothly and rapidly.

I believe a critic aids a writer most by accepting the thrust of the writer's talent and analysing where his powers work and where they are deficient. I have emphasised where Easmon is most effective, but of course his skill is not complete and his book far from perfect. The shift from comedy to a kind of tragedy that he attempts about mid-way through the text is not, as the episode about Banky Vincent is, entirely smooth, and some lurching misdirection is involved. The tragedy of Briwa is actually more like melodrama and therefore not as deep and sharp as it might be. Further, there is a fine line in characterising between capturing the natural inconsistency of any human being and producing a confused or confusing portrait of behaviour. Easmon does not always stay on the correct side of this fine line in the book's two major characterisations. And a few of the book's minor characters seem relatively functionless or virtually unnecessary. This perhaps results from the book's original position as part of a trilogy. None the less, disproportionate space is afforded a few people who really do not add much to the narration, while Makallay's entire adventure in Luawa is omitted. Finally, some of the book's conclusion is so silly that it cannot be taken seriously, and it spoils what should be the sombre mood of Briwa's death. A car roars up with heroes no one knows or cares about, horns hoot while the fire inside crackles, Makallay blandly calls 'That's V.K. my dear. Mahtah, run down and let them in,' while struggling with Chief Briwa. As I have mentioned I believe these parts of the conclusion so bad they do not seem important – a tactical blot quickly forgotten since out of keeping with the rest of the book.

I do not believe it aids a writer to demand that he have the same political views as any particular critic, or that he conceive of Africa in the same manner. A writer's commitment to his talent or art is a difficult enough burden without adding ideological ballast. What the writer thinks about politics or the provinces is generally irrelevant to the artistic success or lack of success his book contains. You cannot

86 increase commitment the way you increase rice production. If you can,

perhaps the OAS should station a commitment expert in each African nation and spare the critics this job. Anyway, perhaps literature truly about life, about real people, cannot avoid being committed. I think the critic owes it to the writer, and the reader, to examine closely what the book says rather than what the critic thinks it should say or what the critic supposes the writer thinks. Criticism may reveal the book a triumph or a flop, but it should reveal the book itself and not the prejudices of the critic.

NOTES

1. Miss Aidoo's note is in the *Legon Observer*, 111, No. 13 (21 June 1968), pp. 17–18. Gerald Moore writes in *African Literature Today*, No. 4.
2. *The Burnt-Out Marriage* is in fact the last part of a trilogy, the rest of which has not been published. Makallay's lover is developed in an earlier section. *Ed.*
3. Dr Easmon asserts that he had no conscious intention of giving the two women a homosexual relationship. *Ed.*

Language and Action in the Novels of Chinua Achebe

Gareth Griffiths

In the final section of *Things Fall Apart* Okonkwo's slaying of the court messenger has brought out the white District Commissioner. He is intent on 'doing justice', but Okonkwo's suicide forestalls him. We are then given two views of the subsequent action, Obierika's and the commissioner's. To the commissioner the inability of Okonkwo's fellow-tribesmen to handle the body of a suicide is fascinating. He is, we are told, 'a student of primitive customs'. Transferred momentarily by the phrase from an 'inside' to an 'outside' view of the action we become aware more decisively than before that the words we have been reading in English are reproducing Ibo thoughts and speech-patterns.

> Obierika, who had been gazing steadily at his friend's dangling body, turned suddenly to the District Commissioner, and said ferociously: 'That man was one of the greatest men in Umuofia. You drove him to kill himself; and now he will be buried like a dog . . .' He could not say more. His voice trembled and choked his words. 'Shut up!' shouted one of the messengers, quite unnecessarily.

88 The command is unnecessary for two reasons. First, because Obierika, overcome by his feelings, *can* say no more; and, secondly, because anything he does say, including the speech he has just made, will be quite incomprehensible to the commissioner who has had to speak 'through an interpreter'. To the commissioner anything that he says sounds like a series of primitive grunts. They are speaking, we recall ironically, in a savage tongue. Through a simple pointing device Achebe can demonstrate the commissioner's exclusion from the society he 'rules'. It is a linguistic exile, and the staple of the novel is language. Achebe can recreate the bitter history of his people through the history of words.

Defeated by the impenetrability of the Ibo world, the commissioner retreats into a language whose register emphasises him as the representative of all those aged colonial administrators who 'know their natives'. His reflections on the scene are preparations for memoir and reminiscence. But what he reflects on is not a memory but an act, not a reminiscence but an experience. The crudity and imperceptiveness of his reflections are set over against the detailed and subtle insights of Achebe's own 'record'.

> As he walked back to the court he thought about that book. Every day brought him some new material. The story of a man who had killed a messenger and then hanged himself would make interesting reading. One could write a whole chapter on him. Perhaps not a whole chapter but a reasonable paragraph, at any rate. There was so much else to include, and one must be firm in cutting out details. He had already chosen the title of the book, after much thought: *The Pacification of the Primitive Tribes of the Lower Niger.*

As Gerald Moore has said, the commissioner's book is inevitable judged against the book we have just read. Achebe has 'gone back to that bleak little paragraph of despised and garbled history.'[1] He has tried to refine the phrases which have clouded the values of tribal life. His vision, this implies, is superior, since it operates from an 'inside' viewpoint which is impossible for the 'student of primitive customs'. But although this is clearly so, the insideness of Achebe's vision can be overstressed. By the very act of writing Achebe's stance is contiguous to that of the commissioner. Both seek to reduce the living, oral world of Umuofia to a series of words on the page; and they are English words, for Achebe as well as for the commissioner. In his attempt to present a picture of the destruction of tribal Iboland Achebe is aware that in gaining the voice to speak he reveals his involvement with the destruction which he records. That is why there is no simple condemnation possible, not for Okonkwo, nor Nwoye, nor even for the commissioner. Neither is there any temptation to sentimentalise. The search is not for a lost idyll, nor **89** an historical excuse, but for a meaningful appraisal of what has been lost and what gained, and a clear analysis of where the writer and his contemporaries stand in the list of residual legatees.

For Achebe the novel is a vehicle of self-discovery. Writing is an activity through which the African can define his identity and re-discover his historical roots. This self-defining function of the novel is, for obvious reasons, especially important to writers in a post-colonial situation, especially where their exposure to European culture has led to an undervaluing of the traditional values and practices. This explains in part the prominence of the autobiography, or autobiographical novel form, in recent African writing. The role of the autobiography, often the first book produced by young African intellectuals, is less to record past experience and evaluate it than to assess the possibilities for future action. The need to determine what I am precedes the possibility of defining what I can be or do. Writers as diverse as Mphalele, Gatheru, Kariuki, Ngugi and Achebe are all, in their various ways, engaged in an investigation of the inherited and acquired characteristics in their cultural make-up. This concern with identity is rooted in the African writer's problem with language. The very choice of language involves him in a deliberate public stance; his use of dialect, or of phrases in his native language, are cultural gests as well as rhetorical devices; while his movement from one register to another in the recording of speech is a direct sociological comment. Inevitably in such a situation the writing of a novel, even more than usual, becomes an act of self-definition. It is Achebe's distinction that he recognises this more clearly than any other African writer, and uses his situation to define the history of his own rhetoric.

Achebe has insisted upon the committed stance of the African writer. He has a clear vision of the duty which the writer owes to his society in a post-colonial situation. The writer's task is primarily to rehabilitate the culture which the colonising culture has overlooked or distorted. In his own words the writer's first duty is to demonstrate:

> that African peoples did not hear of culture for the first time from Europeans; that their societies were not mindless but frequently had a philosophy of great depth and value and beauty, that they had poetry and, above all, they had dignity. (*Nigeria Magazine*, June 1964)

But, paradoxically, it is the legacy of colonialism in the shape of a world-language which the writer must employ to perform this re-habilitation. In Achebe's words, if colonialism did not give the African **90** peoples 'a song, it at least gave them a tongue, for singing'. (*Insight*

Oct./Dec. 1966, p. 20). In setting out to celebrate the traditional African culture Achebe is not blind to its faults. As he says:

> We cannot pretend that our past was one long technicolour idyll. We have to admit that like other people's pasts ours had its good as well as its bad sides. (*Nigeria Magazine*, June 1964)

He celebrates the tribal societies of the past as societies in which human beings face situations with the same tragic inadequacies that men possess in all times. Further, he is aware that as a modern writer he cannot identify totally with the values of the tribal past, since these values are only part of his inheritance, and often conflict with the social and emotional demands which the modern African experience makes upon those who live it.

In *Things Fall Apart* the central character is Okonkwo. But, as the novel develops, we realise that it is Nwoye not Okonkwo who takes the first step that will lead the Ibo writer to be able to record in 'a world-language' the disintegration of his tribal past. Okonkwo's 'success' leads to his destruction, Nwoye's 'failure' ensures his survival in the changing world of Umuofia. The modern African intellectual is the descendant of the tribal underdog, an ironic variation on the theory of social Darwinism which has played such a prominent and derisory role in the colonial view of the Afro-Asian world.

This is a concomitant of the central irony of the book, that Okonkwo is destroyed because he performs more than is expected of him, and sacrifices his personal life to an exaggerated, even pathological, sense of communal duty. This made clear by his over-response to the Oracle's demand that Ikemefuna should be killed, when he ignores the warning of the old man Ezeudu. When such a man advises Okonkwo to moderate his action and he ignores his advice he is acting in defiance of the values of his society, for in Umuofia social values are, literally, in the mouths of the old and the wise.

Nwoye, on the other hand, puts personal feelings above social responsibility. He and Okonkwo's father, to whom he is considered a 'throwback', are more comprehensible to the post-tribal world. In this respect Nwoye's greater capacity for personal relationships and his deeper feelings for personal value is clearly a gain; but one which is accompanied by a loss of pride, of social unity and clarity of purpose. It involves the destruction of the tribe as the unit of value. Nwoye's movement away from the tribal values that Okonkwo defends is the first stage of the journey for the Western-educated Nigerians of Achebe's own generation. Achebe is the inheritor of Nwoye's revolt as well as of Okonkwo's sacrifice. He can celebrate the 'depth and value and beauty' of tribal Ibo **91** culture, but he must do so with the tools gained in the act of destroying it.

Achebe's effect in the final chapter of *Things Fall Apart* is obtained by shifting from the dominant (Umuofian) viewpoint to that of the white intruder. Such a shift is only possible for a man exposed, in some degree, to both cultures. The characteristic effects of Achebe's irony depend on the position which he occupies, poised between two worlds whose interaction he seeks to record. It is Achebe's distinction that he is not content merely to document his situation. He sets out to explore the possibilities it offers for a unique comment on the limitations of the human situation.

Obi Okonkwo in *No Longer at Ease* faces an even more complex situation than that which destroyed his grandfather. But it is a situation which grows from the same basic dilemma. Obi's inability to reconcile his communal responsibilities with his personal life is the reverse image of his grandfather's failure. Like Okonkwo, Obi responds with a tragic, misdirected energy. Unable to accept the solution of the Umuofia Progressive Union and outwit convention, he attempts openly to defy it. He is as over-ready to leap to the image of his emancipation from customary superstition as Okonkwo was to leap to the role of defender of Umuofia. But the final result of his struggle is exposure and imprisonment, when he takes a bribe without observing the necessary caution which the society requires.

The central theme of *No Longer at Ease* is the distance between what is said to be and what is. For example, the morality of public office offered by Mr Green, the white civil servant, is a façade, like the accountant's clean collar in Conrad's *Heart of Darkness*. It asserts an ideal, but one irrelevant to the problems of the time and place; and it is bitterly exposed in Mr Green's tired and cliché-ridden sermons on the effects of the climate on the 'African character'. But equally unacceptable is the UPS President's suggestion that Obi's crime is not that he has accepted a bribe, but that he has not taken 'time to look round first and know what is what'. The proverbial morality of the tribe is no clear guide in this new world, as the language of the UPS members clearly shows.

> The President said it was a thing of shame for a man in the senior service to go to prison for twenty pounds. He repeated twenty pounds, spitting it out. 'I am against people reaping where they have not sown. But we have a saying that if you want to eat a toad you should look for a fat and juicy one.'

92 The relativity of the presidential morality is neatly caught in the shift from the Christian to the Ibo aphorism. Mr Green, the UPS President, and Obi too, are all caught between two worlds, and the language and events of the novel analyse their dilemma with clarity and compassion.

In a recent article in this journal Bernth Lindfors argued that:

> Okonkwo erred by daring to attempt something he did not have the power to achieve; this makes him a tragic hero. Obi erred by stooping to take bribes; this makes him a crook. To put it in proverbial terms: Okonkwo wrestles his chi, Obi swallows a toad. It is not only the stupidity but the contemptibility of Obi's ways that many of the proverbs in the novel help to underscore. [2]

But the process seems to me to be more complex, and the role of the proverbial commentary more ambiguous. It is not only a reduction in the hero we observe, but also a reduction in the scale of the moral universe he moves in. In the proverbial commentary we are aware not only of Obi's inadequacy, but also of the inadequacy of the proverbial culture itself. It no longer provides a valid morality from which Obi's 'crookedness' excludes him. In fact, it is one source of the pressure which makes Obi capitulate to the practice of his time and take bribes. It is this proverbial wisdom on which the UPS draws to justify its demands that Obi acts on behalf of the tribal community. Indeed, it would seem that one of the major functions of this residual tribal organisation is to effect bribes and to obtain posts under false pretences.

> We are not going to ask him to bring his salary to share among us. It is in little things like this that he can help us.

It is to the proverbs that the speaker returns to justify his claim.

> It is our fault if we do not approach him. Shall we kill a snake and carry it in our hand when we have a bag for putting long things in?

Communal loyalty and nepotism can be demonstrated in a single action. The proverbial universe is no longer intact, and so it is insufficient to view Obi's behaviour as a foolish movement from effective communal values to selfish individualism. The choice is outside his control. The communal values have themselves been destroyed, as we see when we view the proverbs in the context of the action. As Gerald Moore has said, commenting on the 'uncertain pomposity' of the UPS President's style of public speaking,

Someone else's words, someone else's values are filling his mouth. All **93** that is Ibo in him is his extravagance and love of status. The proverbs which still occur from time to time in the speech of Achebe's modern characters come out like undigested gobbets. In *Things Fall Apart*, they were both the informing source and the natural expression of the people's thought.[3]

But if the communal universe has fallen apart Obi is equally dissatisfied and ill at ease with his new individualistic values. They are unable to satisfy his continuing need for identity with the life of the past. Thus, although Obi recognises that by the standards of his European education it is right that he should reject the irrational 'osu' taboo, his decision is undermined by the silence with which he greets Clara's confession of her status.

> 'I am an osu,' she wept. Silence. She stopped weeping and quietly disengaged herself from him. Still he said nothing. 'So you see we cannot get married,' she said, quite firmly, almost gaily – a terrible kind of gaiety. Only the tears showed she had wept.
> 'Nonsense!' said Obi. He shouted it almost, as if by shouting now he could wipe away those seconds of silence, when everything had seemed to stop, waiting in vain for him to speak.

However franctically he acts, and however loudly he asserts his 'emancipation' afterwards this initial silence cannot be erased.

Even Obi's father has to admit that the cult-slave taboo is out-dated and unfair when he is reminded by Obi that the Christian ethic deplores such discrimination. He is, after all, that Nwoye who found in the abstract Christian ideals of love and charity his own platform of revolt against the tribal codes. But he has learned from the bitterness of his own experience what Obi has yet to learn, that such a revolt destroys even as it liberates.

> 'Who will marry your daughters? Whose daughters will marry your sons? Think of that my son. We are Christians, but we cannot marry our own daughters.'

This is one of the few points where a clear allusion is made to the events of the previous novel. Isaac/Nwoye tells Obi the story of how his father Okonkwo had slain Ikemefuna, and how as a result he had fled his family with his father's curse on his head. His meaning is improperly understood by Obi. But to the reader it is clear enough. Isaac is trying to tell the crusading Obi that destruction may result not only from evil actions but from those actions we believe to be good. Issues of good and bad are abstractions which men employ to justify their own ponderous **94** and clumsy swings from excess to excess. In this analysis of the clash of standards we see that the Yeatsian dialectic implicit in the title of Achebe's first novel is still active in the world of *No Longer at Ease*.[4] Obi's mother, profoundly unaware of the dilemma which has sent first father and now son 'through fire', plants the opposing pole and completes the circle of destruction:

'. . . if you do this thing while I am alive, you will have my blood on your head, because I shall kill myself . . .'

The issues of right and wrong, of simple moral judgements on individuals, or even simpler explanations in terms of social or historical pressures resolve themselves again into the living tensions of the people who endure them. Once again there is no simple choice between tribal custom and modern progress. Obi's individualist stand is not heroic. The customary and proverbial wisdom of the tribe is not infallible. To satisfy the demands of the world which he has inherited Obi, like his contemporaries, must both change and remain static. It is this painful, and often sordid, condition of tension that Achebe's novels explore.

In his third novel, *Arrow of God*, Achebe returns to the theme of destruction of the tribal world. It is a more complex and ambitious book than the earlier two. It has benefited from the definitions and insights which the two earlier books have provided. With greater confidence and control, and with a deeper assurance, Achebe sets out once again to show in the 'historical process' the inadequacies and limitations with which man confronts the worlds he claims to rule.

Ezeulu, Winterbottom and Oduche, Ezeulu's convert son, are all bound within the limitations of their vision. For Achebe there can be no simple choice between these viewpoints. He is able to step back from his characters and show us the intentions and failures of each: Winterbottom's well-intentioned but destructive 'paternalism'; Oduche's desperate attempt to come to terms with 'the ambivalence of his present life'; and Ezeulu's struggle to determine what is possible for a man driven by the events of life and the whims of the god he serves. Even in Ezeulu's tragic struggle there is no final solution, for the writer, as Achebe knows, is involved with the kind of self-consciousness which overthrows the gestures it celebrates. Okonkwo's suicide and Obi's imprisonment gesticulate towards an idea of fate as confusion and puzzled inadequacy, but in Ezeulu's madness Achebe finds his most powerful symbol of the limitations of men.

At any other time Ezeulu would have been more than equal to his grief. He would have been equal to any grief not compounded with humiliation. Why, he asked himself again and again, why had Ulu **95** chosen to deal thus with him, to strike him down and cover him with mud? What was his offence? Had he not divined the god's will and obeyed it? When was it ever heard that a child was scalded by the piece of yam its own mother put into its palm? What man would send his son with a potsherd to bring fire from a neighbour's hut and then unleash rain? Whoever sent his son up the palm to gather nuts and then took an axe and felled the tree? But today such a thing had happened before the eyes of all. What could it point to but the collapse and ruin of all things? Then a god, finding himself powerless, might take to his heels and in one final, backward glance at his abandoned worshippers cry:

> If the rat cannot flee fast enough
> Let him make way for the tortoise!

Perhaps it was the constant, futile throbbing of these thoughts that finally left a crack in Ezeulu's mind. Or perhaps his implacable assailant having stood over him for a little while stepped on him as on an insect and crushed him in the dust. But this final malevolence proved merciful. It allowed Ezeulu, in his last days, to live in the haughty splendour of a demented high priest and spared him knowledge of the final outcome.

Bernth Lindfors argues that the 'proverbial commentary' condemns Ezeulu by showing that he has failed to act 'appropriately and responsibly'. But if we view the proverbial devices not in isolation but as part of a total linguistic structure then the 'choice' they offer seems less adequate than Lindfors suggests. Viewed in context we see that Achebe offers more than one explanation:('Perhaps . . . or perhaps . . .')The first takes up the suggestion, developed in many places in the book by the proverbial commentary that Ezeulu has fallen because he has failed to act within the bounds of the 'reasonable' and the 'sensible' in responding to the threat of the white man. The proverbs debate the wisdom of the central decision to send Oduche to learn the white man's power. But significantly the same proverbial wisdom – 'The man who brings ant-ridden faggots into his hut should not grumble when lizards begin to pay him a visit' – is used both by the elders to criticise Ezeulu's policy of sending Oduche to learn the white man's power, and by him to criticise their earlier policy of submission to the initial invasion of Umuaro. (pp. 177–8 and 163 respectively, as Lindfors notes.) At the end of the novel this relativity still appertains, only heightened to a tragic level in its effect. Ezeulu, throughout, has acted according to the truth as he sees it. The psychological insight which Achebe brings to the actions make them more than mere gestures. He establishes that Ezeulu is, in a large-measure, stiff-necked and uncompromising, but there is no suggestion of
hypocrisy in his belief that in all his actions he has been merely 'an

arrow in the bow of his god'. After his son's death Ezeulu's grief and distraction drive him to test the purity of his motives against the one source of truth outside personal feeling available to him. Frantically he runs through the proverbial wisdom seeking for a clear sign that the relationship of trust which must exist between high priest and god still endures. But the guide is no longer reliable. It is the 'constant futile throbbing' of the proverbs echoing mockingly through his brain which, in part, drives him insane. Like the great ceremonial drums which Ezeulu mounts to celebrate the feasts of Ulu the language of the tribe shakes to pieces the conviction and sanity of its chief celebrant. The search is futile, the passage goes on to suggest, because the moral universe of the proverbs with its sequence of appropriate actions and responses has disintegrated along with the society which produced it. It has collapsed in the face of the irresistible and incomprehensible force of the white man, a force blind to the values and meanings of tribal life. This irresistible and incomprehensible force, captured appropriately enough in an allusion resonant with the preoccupations of European culture,[5] is the paradigm for that blind and implacable fate which steps on Ezeulu as on an insect. The role of the white man in the destruction of the tribal world is conceived as much symbolically as historically. And so, Lindfors' conclusion that Ezeulu 'goes too far and plunges himself and his people into disaster' seems an inadequate way of expressing what, examined as a whole, reveals itself as a complex symbol for 'the utmost that we know. Both of ourselves and of the universe'.

The proverbial patterning of the novels does much more than 'evoke the cultural milieu in which the action takes place' (Lindfors). It is a flexible and subtle device which, particularly in the later novels, often serves to define ironically the inappropriateness and dislocation of the characters' responses. If we view it as a continuing pattern of valid judgement on the actions of the novel we will fail to see the ways in which Achebe defines the confusion and loss of identity which accompanies social change. Increasingly in the novels the theme of uprootedness and disorientation is defined through the gap between language and action. An example is the case of the proverb cited by Lindfors in a list of those embodying a comment or warning 'against foolish and unworthy actions':

'Shall we kill a snake and carry it in our hand when we have a bag for putting long things in?'

Clearly, in the context, the proverb does not warn against foolish or **97** unworthy actions, in fact it is used by the old man at the Umofia Progressive Union to justify an unworthy action, or rather to justify an action which in terms of the tribal code is acceptable but in terms of the public morality to which Obi's position exposes him is a crime. To understand the full effect of Achebe's use of proverbial language, or indeed, of any single rhetorical device in his writing, we have to view it as part of an ordered and unified artistic structure. Proverbial language is not a static repository of wisdom to which Achebe subscribes unquestioningly, and against which he measures the actions of his novels in an uncritical way. Rather it is one of a range of rhetorical devices which serve to define response in a world in which increasingly all response is relative and inadequate. As a writer seeking to define the interaction of two cultures Achebe needs more than a single linguistic standard by which to define the moral dilemma of his characters. The novels explore the growing inadequacy of the proverbial language to function effectively in a world whose demands are phrased in directly opposed terms. But, as Odili Samalu makes clear, a mechanical mastery of the new terminology is no more adequate than a parrot-like command of the old.

A Man of the People is something of an intrusion into the steady flow of Achebe's novels. Nigerian reviewers hailed it as a sign of Achebe's new 'commitment'. But to regard it as marking a *volte face* in Achebe's work is to ignore the continuity it has with earlier preoccupations and procedures. Nevertheless, it does mark a major technical innovation, since it is the first of the novels to omit the direct intervention of the narrator. The onus which this places on the reader to judge the reliability of the central character makes it more vital than ever that we recognise the inadequacy of relying on any single rhetorical procedure as a 'grammar of values' by which to judge the events of the book. If we believe with Lindfors that Odili Samalu is a man whose 'clear vision provides an undistorted view of a warped society' then we can read the book as an indictment of a world in which Odili, the hero, is sacrificed to the wicked chiefs Nanga and Koko. But to read the novel in this way is to ignore not only the multiple distinctions between what Odili does and what he says, but also between what he says and how he says it. As Arthur Ravenscroft has said, Odili Samalu is:

> both serious accuser and comically self-accused in the rotten society of *A Man of the People*. It isn't simply a matter of contrast between Odili's words and his performance, but a question of how the words themselves reveal a shallow personality: the smirking, familiar, I-know-what-I'm-talking-about tone of so many TV commentators.[6]

It is this level of comment we miss if we concentrate too exclusively on the proverbial commentary as the controlling rhetorical device. The proverbial comment is an important guide which Achebe uses to pinpoint the dangers and difficulties accompanying moral choice, and to comment on the reliability of his characters' responses. But it is one amongst many, and is often used not to establish a grammar of values but to comment ironically on the discrepancies between the solutions of the tribal past and the problems of the urban present. For example, at the end of the novel there occurs an example of a proverb which has echoed through the entire book; the proverb 'that some one has taken enough for the owner to see' is here applied to the urban offences of the Nangas and Kokos. In the society of the villages it represents a meaningful ideal of tolerance, an effective standard which sets a limit to the natural dishonesty of man. It recognises that men will always rob other men, and that the real offence is to take more than the owner can afford to lose. As an expression of a semi-communal society where personal property is not sacred, since the pattern of life does not force men to compete with one another for survival, it is effective and meaningful. But when transferred to the 'dog eat dog' world of Nanga and Koko it becomes a useless and dangerous piece of sophistry.

> 'Koko had taken enough for the owner to see,' said my father. My father's words struck me because they were the same words the villagers of Anata had spoken of Josiah, the abominated trader. Only in their case the words had meaning. The owner was the village, and the village had a mind; it could say no to sacrilege. But in the affairs of the nation there was no owner, the laws of the village become powerless.

As with the laws of the village, so with the language in which those laws find expression. After all, we recall, Odili's father is referring to the death of Max, which has deprived Eunice of more than she can overlook ... her lover. As Odili recognises, a different morality applies, embodied in a different language:

> Max was avenged not by the people's collective will but by one woman who loved him.

The single most important technique of *A Man of the People* is not the proverbial patterning but the superbly controlled distance established between the reader and Odili Samalu. Odili sees more clearly than any other character the gap between what is said and what is in the world around him. He struggles, as far as he is able, to act up to the ideals he proposes, but despite his intentions he is betrayed time and **99** time again into self-deception and hypocrisy. He tells his story defensively, as if half-aware of his plight, and organises his material and his comment to justify his action and its outcome. But his efforts only serve to emphasise the gap between intention and achievement. We are simultaneously made aware of the double-standards he operates when judging his own actions and those of others, and of the tragic innocence necessary to continue such self-deceptions successfully. Obi Okonkwo in *No Longer at Ease* was used by Achebe to explore the dilemma of the young Nigerian trapped by the conflicting demands of two worlds, exiled from both the traditional and the contemporary solutions; Odili is a victim of the same dilemma, but now Achebe has deliberately withdrawn his own articulacy, and capacity for honest self-appraisal. The result is an ironic novel of high distinction the achievement of which rests firmly on Achebe's ability to make his technique an instrument of discovery.

This technique is firmly rooted in Achebe's manipulation of the wide range of 'languages' available to him to define Odili's world. He has access to more than a single proverbial source of comment. He has available a whole series of 'languages', from the 'literary' European English register to the untranslated Ibo phrase. The selection of the appropriate register is not merely a question of accurate representation and effective documentation but also of rhetorical appropriateness.

For example, he outlines the range of possibilities when he shows Odili trying to get a clear picture of the Nanga household, and their speech-habits.

> A small thing, but it struck me even as early as this: Mr Nanga always spoke English or pidgin; his children, whom I discovered went to expensive private schools run by European ladies spoke impeccable English, but Mrs Nanga stuck to our language – with the odd English word thrown in now and again.

Ironically, Achebe can now demonstrate how the scale of values implicit in these speech-habits are reversed when one attempts to construct a convention for representing them all in English. Thus Mrs Nanga whom we remember is too 'bush' for her husband's new position speaks in a fairly standard English. How else is one to represent standard Ibo? But her husband, the Minister of Culture, often speaks in pidgin, the mark of his 'successful' detribalisation and social advancement. The choice of languages comments with devastating irony on the effect which the 'civilising' process has had on the native African culture, a culture despised by Nanga's children who speak 'impeccable English'.

Apparently the Minister insisted that his children must be taken home to their village at least once a year.

'Very wise,' I said.

'Without it,' said Mrs Nanga, 'they would become English people. Don't you see they hardly speak our language? Ask them something in it and they reply in English. The little one, Micah, called my mother "a dirty bush woman".'

In *Arrow of God* Achebe had investigated similar ironies exposed by the peculiar insight gained in reporting the African world through an 'outside' language. For example, in the scene in which the kotma – a pidgin corruption of court messenger – demonstrates to the Umuarians the linguistic advantages of being civilised. The two messengers have arrived at Ezeulu's hut in order to arrest him, only to discover that he has already set out to answer Winterbottom's summons and that they have passed him on the road.

'What does he look like?' asked the corporal.

'He is as tall as an iroko tree and his skin is white like the sun. In his youth he was called Nwa-anyanwu.'

'And his son?'

'Like him. No difference.'

The two policemen conferred in the white man's tongue to the great admiration of the villagers.

'Sometine na dat two porson we cross for road,' said the corporal.

'Sometine na dem,' said his companion. 'But we no go return back jus like dat. All dis waka wey we waka come her no fit go for nating.'

The corporal thought about it. The other continued: 'Sometine na lie dem de lie, I no wan make dem put trouble for we head . . .'

He addressed them in Ibo:

'We think you are telling us a lie, and so we must make quite sure otherwise the white man will punish us. What we shall do then is to take two of you – handcuffed – to Okperi.'

As a moment's reflection makes clear the irony depends upon all the language being English, so that when Achebe shifts from pidgin to Ibo he does so by shifting from a fractured and half-digested English to a rich and subtle version of the same language. The rich and subtle language is the savage speech of Umuaro.

In *A Man of the People* yet another level of language is discovered, and turned to account. This is the language to which Odili aspires, and which serves as the main vehicle of his distancing in the book. In its own way it is as half-digested and false as the kotma's pidgin. It leans heavily on redundant metaphors and the clichés of second-rate fiction; **101**

Odili, we recall, has literary ambitions amongst others. It is this language which undermines the confidence which the reader has in Odili's reliability as a narrator. Take, for example, his account of the first time he 'slept with' Elsie:

> Elsie was, and for that matter still is, the only girl I met and slept with the same day – in fact within an hour. I know that faster records exist and am not entering this one for that purpose, nor am I trying to prejudice anyone against Elsie. I only put it down because that was the way it happened. It was during my last term at the University and, having as usual put off my revision to the last moment, I was having a rough time. But one evening there was a party organised by the Student's Christian Movement and I decided in spite of my arrears of work to attend and give my brain time to cool off. I am not usually lucky, but that evening I was. I saw Elsie standing in a group with other student nurses and made straight for her. She turned out to be a most vivacious girl newly come to the nursing school. We danced twice . . .

The reader's initial distrust is sparked off by the clichés, and the self-conscious slickness of the phrasing: 'for that matter still is', 'in fact within', 'the way it happened', 'having a rough time', 'time to cool off', 'made straight for her', 'most vivacious'. These draw our attention to a more radical falsity in the self-justifying and swaggering tone that Odili adopts. Even before he begins the story of his relationship with Elsie he has adopted a defensive stance: 'I . . . am not entering', 'nor am I trying to prejudice'. Of course, the denials only make it even clearer that this is exactly what he is trying to do. Later in the novel, when Elsie is taken from him by Chief Nanga, Odili is bitter and morally indignant. But, as this passage makes clear, Elsie's later 'faults' are the virtues which first attract him to her, vivaciousness and attainability.

When Odili meets the American public relations expert whose brief is to advise the government on the best way of selling its image to America he is exposed to the logical end of the journey from language to lie.

> 'So you see, Mr . . . I'm sorry I didn't catch your first name?'
> 'Odili.'
> 'Odili – a beautiful sound – may I call you by that?'
> 'Sure,' I said, already partly Americanised.
> 'Mine is John. I don't see why we should call one another Mister this and Mister that – like the British.'
> 'Nor do I,' I said.
> 'What I was saying,' he went on, 'is that we do not pretend to be perfect. But we have made so much progress lately that I see no cause for anyone to despair. What is important is that we must press on.

We must not let up. We just must not be caught sleeping on the switch again . . .'

I was still savouring the unusual but, I thought, excellent technological imagery when I heard as though from far-away John's voice make what I call an astounding claim . . .

The claim towards which the whole conversation has been skilfully leading is that America is the only nation to have had the power to conquer others and to refrain from doing so. Odili is bemused by the new language, by its unfamiliarity and the new vistas it opens up of a world in which the problems of men can be solved if only we pay sufficient attention to our switches, and is unable to refute the argument, though he does not believe it. He has been exposed to a master of the rhetoric which he himself employs in his little self-deceptions, and which Nanga too uses to fool his electorate. When Nanga uses the phrase 'national cake' to describe the rights of his compatriots to a share in the posts of government we observe the same process operating.

The hackneyed phrase 'national cake' was getting to some of us for the first time, and so it was greeted with applause. 'Owner of book!' cried one admirer, assigning in those three brief words the ownership of the white man's language to the Honourable Minister, who turned round and beamed on the speaker.

Just as with the kotma in *Arrow of God*, we are distanced from the reaction of the villager to Nanga's 'command of' the English language through the registers of language in which admirer and admired operate. Odili, too, seems to be distanced as we are, and to share our sense of the irony. But this is not entirely true. The phrase 'getting to some of us' suggests that Odili's insight is the product of hindsight, and that he is laying claim to a perceptiveness which at the time he did not possess. So we react not only to the falsity of Nanga's world, but also to the falsity of Odili's claim to be outside the Nanga values. Like a set of Chinese-boxes Achebe operates the shades and nuances which separate the worlds of words that make up his inheritance.

Odili is not a deliberate hypocrite. He develops in the course of the novel, and makes often courageous attempts to find a workable morality which will bridge the gap between his ideals and the shifting morass of ideas and standards he has inherited. The pathetic, and often comic, convolutions that this involves him in reflect the difficulties which face him and his contemporaries. Odili sees the way in which Nanga and Koko can exploit the failure of the old moral code:

'Let them eat,' was the people's opinion . . . 'if you survive, who knows? it may be your turn to eat tomorrow.'

He sees too that until men have been out of the rain long enough 'to be able to say "To hell with it"' there is no hope of impartiality and principle in political life. In fact, he sees more clearly than anyone else in the novel what is wrong, but his analysis is useless because he shares the very faults which destroy those around him. He brings to his actions a pettiness and a hypocritical pride which prevent him from distinguishing between his private satisfactions and his public hopes. What Odili lacks is the detachment to see his own faults as clearly as he sees those of the people around him. At the end of the novel, he comments bitterly that:

> You died a good death if your life had inspired someone to come forward and shoot your murderer in the chest without asking to be paid.

It is a conclusion which fails to satisfy. From Eunice's act there is no way through to reality. It remains a blind gesture of personal retaliation, quite incomprehensible to the world in which it occurs.

> She stood like a stone figure, I was told, for some minutes more. Then she opened her handbag as if to take out a handkerchief, took out a pistol instead and fired two bullets into Chief Koko's chest. Only then did she fall on Max's body and begin to weep like a woman; and then the policemen seized her and dragged her away. A *very strange girl*, people said.[7]

A Man of the People is Achebe's first attempt completely to disassociate himself from the solutions and figures he creates. But it is a logical technique for a man whose work as a whole shows the finest kind of objectivity. The need for such objectivity, so amply illustrated by Odili Samalu, is the product of the dilemma which Achebe faces by being isolated from a simple allegiance to any one culture. At the end of this novel the military coup offers a temporary relief, but there is no evidence that they will not prove to be merely the latest residents to barricade themselves within the house of government. The irony of Odili's account of the elevation of Max to Hero of the Revolution makes it clear that this is no simple Golden Age which is being ushered in. If any solution is proposed, it is that political and moral life will remain that of 'you chop, meself I chop, palaver finish' until the kind of detachment and objectivity which guides this novel becomes a possibility for the nation at large. That a Nigerian artist has shown himself capable of this is the most tangible sign of hope.

NOTES

1. Gerald Moore, *Seven African Writers,* Three Crowns Books, Oxford University Press, 1962, p. 65.
2. Bernth Lindfors, 'The Palm Oil with which Achebe's words are eaten', *African Literature Today*, No. 1, 1968.
3. Gerald Moore, *op. cit.,* p. 70.
4. See 'Yeats and Achebe', A. G. Stock, *Journal of Commonwealth Literature*, July 1968, No. 5.
5. The image recalls the final image of Hardy's *Tess.*
6. *Journal of Commonwealth Literature*, No. 6, January 1969, pp. 122–3.
7. My stress.

The Traditional Content of the Plays of Wole Soyinka

Oyin Ogunba

*The first half of this article appeared
in African Literature Today No. 4, p.2*

The traditional festival model for *A Dance of the Forests* is not as clear-cut as in *Kongi's Harvest* and *The Strong Breed*, the two plays discussed earlier. Deliberate experimentation appears to be more thoroughgoing here than in the other two plays and one is tempted to think that this is a special Wole Soyinka festival. Nevertheless, the idea of the welcoming of the dead, the illustrious ancestors, and the coming to the city of old and forgotten relatives does suggest a Yoruba Egungun festival.

But this is an Egungun festival with a difference, because the spirits of health and the illustrious ancestors expected, are forestalled and their place is taken by malevolent gods and evil spirits. It is as if on the National Day of a country, when everything is set for a great and triumphant celebration, foreign troops suddenly break the border, take over control, offering destruction and death to the population. Aroni who boasts that he is responsible for this costly trick on the human community is here in the role of a perfidious officer who betrays trust.

But he is also in his full traditional role of the ubiquitous, mischievous, all-knowing spirit. Aroni's *oriki* (praise name) is:

'Aroni gbe'le, gbe'gbe, gb'oko, gbe'ju, gbe'gi.'
'Aroni who dwells in the house, in the bush, in the forests, in the wilderness, in fact, everywhere.'

Aroni is a timeless spirit who knows the past with astonishing intimacy and can look far into the future. With such disturbing knowledge it is difficult for him genuinely to share in the false joy of the human community on this occasion or collaborate with them to produce illustrious ancestors. He knows that the gods are not well-disposed to humanity and that in particular Ogun and Eshuoro will, as ever, dominate human thought, producing large-scale disaster and death. Ogun and Eshuoro are Yoruba gods. Ogun is the god of iron, war and everything that has to do with steel. Eshuoro is the god of wariness and chance.

One is tempted to say that the author and Aroni are one and the same character in this play and that Soyinka is here both a historian and a prophet. As a historian he appears to be intensely aware of the immutable principle of violence and its triumph in human affairs. He probably will not go as far as his counterpart, the historian of the play to advocate this violence. But he seems to be in sympathy with the notion that:

'War is the only consistency that past ages afford us. It is the legacy which new nations seek to perpetuate. Patriots are grateful for wars. Soldiers have never questioned bloodshed. The cause is always the accident your Majesty and war is the Destiny.'

As a prophet he may have foreseen with remarkable exactitude that this young nation, this gathering of the tribes (*A Dance of the Forests* is Nigeria's Independence play) will soon, like the half-child, lose the game of peace and get plunged in an internecine strife.

Here too, as in *Kongi's Harvest*, the apparently joyous atmosphere of a festival is used to proclaim the fact that there is nothing really to rejoice about, that the past has been one of opportunism and crime and that the future is going to be bleak with suffering and death on an enormous scale. So the festival is 'averted' and *A Dance of the Forests* which sets out as a dance of creation or rebirth rapidly becomes a dance of death. The half-child (abiku) plays his game and loses all. A genuinely good creation is impossible because this young nation cannot really escape the heritage of universal crime. The Abiku – the progeny of violence and unscrupulous self-interest cannot survive because its mortality is inherent and basic. The idea of the Abiku as a symbol of the life **107** and death of nations is, in fact, particularly appropriate – for both the symbol and its referent share the element of the inscrutable. *Abiku* who is described as a half-child is, in fact, a no-child, that is, a child that is born to die at infancy.

The full impact of Wole Soyinka's traditional setting in *A Dance of the Forests* is to create a disenchantment with traditional glory. Here is a past full of crime and a present dominated by the inveterate enmity of Ogun and Eshuoro. The despair of the play is that the future will be based on this uncertain foundation and will be equally hopeless.

Apart from the overall design of a festival in the three plays treated above, in some other plays specific traditional sanctions are examined and their values or validity tested. Such is the idea of sacred land in *The Swamp Dwellers* and that of traditional wisdom in *The Lion and the Jewel*. *The Swamp Dwellers* explores the theme of man's misfortune set against hostile nature – physical and human. Here in the swamps land is scarce and man is hard put to it to make a living out of the land. And recently many people, like Awuchike, 'got sick of this place and went to the city'. Makuri summarises the growing depression and restiveness thus:

> 'Those were the days . . . those days were really good. Even when times were harsh and the swamp overran the land, we were able to laugh with the Serpent . . . but these young people . . . They were no sooner born than they want to get out of the village as if it carried a plague . . . I bet none of them has ever taken his wench into the swamps.'

In this place unpitying nature laughs at man's effort, offering him just a tiny parcel of land and then vitiating his honest endeavours by taking away what he has struggled to achieve.

This is the plight of Igwezu, the unsuccessful son of Makuri who too has gone to the city like Awuchike to forget nature's harshness in his home. But in the city too he has been unsuccessful and, running into debt, hopes to make good on the land he has sown before leaving for the city. The disappointment on his home-coming sharpens his grief.

The main point of Igwezu when he confronts the priest, Kadiye, is seriously to question the validity of certain traditional sanctions in the face of inexorable economic facts. While Igwezu starves and virtually loses confidence in his manhood and every other member of the community suffers from malnutrition, the Kadiye, who as a priest of the Serpent should keep the vow of poverty, on the contrary, grows robust. Igwezu's grief loosens his tongue and provokes him to 'sacrilegious' outbursts. He proceeds as if in a cross-examination:

IGWEZU: Who must appease the Serpent of the Swamps?
KADIYE: The Kadiye.
IGWEZU: Who takes the gifts of the people in order that the *beast* may be *gorged* and made *sleepy-eyed* with the feast of sacrifice?
KADIYE: The Kadiye.
IGWEZU: . . . On whom does the land depend for the benevolence of the *reptile*? Tell me that, priest. Answer in one word.
KADIYE: Kadiye.
IGWEZU: Can you see my mask, priest? Is it of this village?
KADIYE: Yes.

. . . .

IGWEZU: Does it sing with the rest? Cry with the rest? Does it till the swamps with the rest of the tribe?
KADIYE: Yes.
IGWEZU: And so that the Serpent might not *vomit* at the wrong season and drown the land, so that he might not swallow at the wrong moment and *gulp* down the unwary traveller, do I not offer my goats to the priest?
KADIYE: Yes.

As this goes on, Igwezu accuses the Kadiye of merely eating up what was intended for sacrifice to the Serpent. Makuri, Igwezu's father, seeing the development of the questioning makes an effort to save the situation. But this fails and Igwezu is driven to the really devastating comments:

IGWEZU: And when the Kadiye blessed my marriage, and tied the heaven-made knot, did he not promise a long-life? Did he not promise children? Did he not promise happiness?
KADIYE: (Did not reply this time.)
IGWEZU: (Slowly and disgustedly.) Why are you so fat, Kadiye?

. . . . .

IGWEZU: I think perhaps you did not slay the fatted calf.
MAKURI: Unsay it, my son. Unsay that at once.
IGWEZU: Kadiye, perhaps you did not slay the fatted calf . . .
MAKURI: May heaven forgive what has been uttered here tonight. May earth reject the folly spoken by my son.
IGWEZU: You lie upon the land, Kadiye, and choke it in the folds of your flesh . . .

Much of Igwezu's comment, of course, expresses the bewilderment of failure and he is later to wonder what power goaded him on. But much of it also indicates the growing contempt he begins to feel for the Serpent of the Swamps. All the epithets used in describing the Serpent in this passage have pejorative connotations. First it is called a 'beast' which is 'gorged' and 'sleepy-eyed'. This means that the Serpent is a **109** glutton revelling in sheer plenitude. The Serpent also 'vomits', presumably as a result of over-feeding or indigestion arising out of a habitual, indiscriminate feasting. This 'reptile' is also equally indiscriminate in its other actions, 'gulping down', the unwary traveller.

For Igwezu the traditional sanctions no longer have a strict hold and the Serpent is discredited for ever. Although he still asks:

> 'If I slew the fatted calf, Kadiye, do you think that the land might breathe again.'

This is more in continuation of the scepticism than a genuine feeling of renewed confidence in the Serpent.

There is thus an unmistakable atheistic tone in *The Swamp Dwellers*. Nature merely sits by and allows man to go through unnecessary suffering, sometimes even smiling at man's misfortunes. Nature, then, is here not a healer, for neither the Beggar who has come from the far north nor Igwezu who has returned dejected from the city finds any consolation whatever in this rural environment; on the contrary they find their ebbing spirit further dampened. Here, nature is a monster devouring relentlessly and indiscriminately.

The image of the Serpent in *The Swamp Dweller* can be given a two-fold explanation. First, there is the idea of the Serpent in traditional African thinking as the original owner, the landlord of the swamps whose tenant the human community is and who therefore demands sacrifice and veneration *de jure*. In this role the Serpent can be a benevolent spirit, though often capricious. Secondly, there is the more universal idea of the Serpent as a creature of prey, a malicious trickster and an enemy – physically and spiritually – to man, for the Serpent misleads man into false hopes and expectations only to betray him at the crucial time. It looks as if this author deliberately combines these two elements – the capricious landlord and the inveterate enemy -- in this particular Serpent in order to emphasise man's predicament. Noticeable here too is an aspect of Wole Soyinka's iconoclasm which calls, almost in the manner of the Kalabari Ekine cult, for a clean break with whatever god gets too proud to the extent of oppressing man. (See Robin Horton 'The Kalabari Ekine Society', *Africa*, Vol. 33, No. 2, 1963, pp. 94–114.)

Igwezu's devastating comment on the Kadiye:

> 'You lie upon the land, Kadiye, and choke it in the folds of your flesh.'

may also carry a secondary meaning. Apart from the obvious surface meaning of sleeping on the land to choke it, it may also mean, with a deliberate ambiguity on the word *lie*, that the Kadiye also tells lies to the people about the true nature of the Serpent. The Kadiye may even be the Serpent itself – as indeed he wears a large tattoo of the Serpent. In that case it is he and the whole bunch of preceding priests who lie on the land, choke it, prevent necessary development and tell lies to the people about the 'divine' wish of the Serpent.

Thus human, far more than physical, nature is the real culprit of men's misfortunes in *The Swamp Dwellers*. Self-interest, disguised in traditional ritual and religious sanctions, encumbers the ground and keeps the people just above starvation level and so makes them perpetually subservient to the Serpent. The tone of despair which has been noticeable from the very start gets more pronounced towards the end especially as it becomes certain that Igwezu's voice of protest will be isolated. The Kadiye will stir up the whole village against this 'sacrilege'. Thus tradition receives a rude shock, but it is momentary and the community soon returns to its age-old sanctions. And so 'the oil-lamps go out slowly and completely' to show the extinction of reason and the re-assertion of ponderous tradition.

One play of Wole Soyinka in which the traditional element is likely to be misunderstood is *The Lion and the Jewel*. In this play, an aspect of modernism in Africa is defeated by tradition with such a delightful ease that one is led to wonder momentarily if this author is not in the Negritude camp. Lakunle, twenty-three, the village school-teacher of Ilujinle has ideas about transforming the village from a mere tradition-bound community into an ultra-modern society. In this he fancies that he is the direct opposite of Baroka, the *bale* (chief) of the village whom he regards as the arch-enemy of progress. Lakunle is also in love with Sidi, the village beauty whom he hopes to bring up into a sophisticated city woman in much the same way as the Ilujinle of his dream.

With such an interesting programme Lakunle should ordinarily win our sympathy. Our main concern, then, is to see how he goes about it. He opposes Baroka's voluptuousness and self-interest and he is quite certain that it is his licentious leisure which is the greatest obstacle to progress. He also advises Sidi to dress in a more modest manner, to stop exposing her breast in the traditional way. Above all, he makes up his mind that he would not pay the bride price. To the bewildered Sidi he says:

'Ignorant girl, can you not understand?
To pay the price would be
To buy a heifer off the market stall
You'd be my chattel, my mere property.'

Very quickly, we realise that the main point about Lakunle is his complete rejection of traditional African ways and equally indiscriminate acceptance of foreign ones. He insists on carrying Sidi's pail of water and later her bundle of firewood in a most un-African way which profoundly shocks her. He delights in kissing her and calls it 'the way of civilised romance' whereas to Sidi it is 'this strange unhealthy mouthing'. He continually talks of a great future for both of them in a way which makes her feel that he is a mere idle dreamer or an incorrigible bookworm.

Lakunle is the platonic lover, a concept quite foreign to Sidi's traditional sensibility. It is quite in character for her to think of Lakunle as an ineffectual lover, a eunuch. For what real man would be content to merely talk of a future when Sidi's lush body craves for an immediate and intense present. In Sidi's traditional way of thinking no real man would make himself the slave of a mere girl and offer to carry her load. Nor would a real man be satisfied with performing 'unhealthy mouthings' when the whole body was at his disposal.

Lakunle's eloquence is also not the type to impress the traditional Sidi, for it is a kind of verbosity easily associated with the eunuch. In certain African communities (for example among the Yoruba) a man who talks too much especially in the company of women and indulges in some childish frolics with them is sometimes regarded as impotent. Objecting to the bride price Lakunle exclaims:

> LAKUNLE: A savage custom, barbaric, outdated,
>   Rejected, denounced, accursed
>   Excommunicated, archaic, degrading
>   Humiliating, unspeakable, redundant
>   Retrogressive, remarkable, unpalatable.
> SIDI: Is the bag empty? Why did you stop?

Sidi's terse reply is full of all the contempt one feels for a mere talker. By revelling so much in words instead of significant action Lakunle fills her with disgust instead of admiration. No wonder she says that Lakunle is a mere 'book-nourished shrimp', a 'no-man' who would not even survive his honeymoon, unlike the vigorous Baroka who is still virile at sixty-two. Sidi has all the time waited in vain for this manifestation of vigour in Lakunle. She wants to accommodate his life-giving virility within her warm body and thrive on this musty fruitfulness as other village belles have done before her. Since this is not forthcoming his rejection is bound to be only a matter of time. For Sidi this 'way of civilised romance' can never be a substitute for the richness of vigorous union.

112   It would be strange if Lakunle is not rejected at Ilujinle, especially by

the unsophisticated Sidi: he looks the type who gets rejected in virtually all communities in spite of his good intentions. Within the context of today's Africa he represents a mere travesty of modernism, an angry young man who wants a change overnight and rushes into action with characteristic temerity. In the end he fails and is left derelict.

One important aspect of Lakunle's make-up, which is also a feature of his indiscriminate acceptance of modernism, is that he is not a clear thinker. He easily mixes trash with substance. In one of his long speeches he lists his programme of activities. We may call this his manifesto:

'[with conviction] Within a year or two I swear
This town shall see a transformation
Bride price will be a thing forgotten
And wives shall take their place by men.
A motor road will pass this spot
And bring the city ways to us.
We'll buy saucepans for all the women
Clay pots are crude and unhygienic
No man shall take more wives than one
That's why they're impotent too soon.
The ruler shall ride cars, not horses
Or a bicycle at the very least.
We'll burn the forest, cut the trees
Then plant a modern park for lovers
We'll print newspapers every day
With pictures of seductive girls.
The world will judge our progress by
The girls that win beauty contests.
While Lagos builds new factories daily
We only play "ayo" and gossip.
Where is our school of Ballroom dancing?
Who here can throw a cocktail party?
We must be modern with the rest
Or live forgotten by the world
We must reject the palm-wine habit
And take to tea, with milk and sugar.'

The author's ironic intention becomes extremely pungent in the last two lines which expose Lakunle's naïvety in thinking that he can, at a stroke, replace established tradition with a *tabula rasa* on which modern ways will be systematically inscribed.

Thus in *The Lion and the Jewel* tradition triumphs and one aspect of modernism is made to sound so ludicrous. But this is not to be regarded necessarily as the author's vote for tradition. One cannot on this victory construct a theory of the author's idealisation of tradition. What he does **113** rather, is to create a caricature of a so-called modern man in order to ridicule some of the crazy notions of the modern African. It looks as if Baroka's triumph is by default deriving from Lakunle's clumsiness and ineffectuality rather than the inherent strength of his position. He is as much the object of the author's scathing satire as Lakunle. His world cannot survive intact for long in spite of the sporadic outbursts of cultural rehabilitation on the African continent by genuine cultivators or tradition-mongers. But the pace of the change cannot be forced given traditional man's innate conservatism.

Lakunle as an agent of modernism fails – has to fail – because for him change is a romantic idea, a dream rather than a feasible reality to be given intelligent construction. As Lakunle fades off we are left with Baroka, the so-called arch-traditionalist who, in spite of appearance, is ready to learn and carry through some of the necessary change. He, at least, will be quite sane and his words in wooing Sidi are reassuring:

'I do not hate progress, only its nature
Which makes all roofs and faces look the same'

and later in the same speech:

'Does sameness not revolt your being
My daughter?'

Baroka will, of course, progress in a manner to please himself first and foremost, but that is the price the community will pay for the failure of its more learned men who are enthusiasts of change without being realists.

Lakunle appears to be a representative of the first generation of the new elite in Africa who are now, happily, dead or superseded. His eloquence – or rather a debasement of eloquence – belongs to the 1930s and 1940s. His new found 'wisdom', that is, his contempt for all African traditions, is a heritage of the nineteenth century when people were systematically encouraged to regard all things African as savage and barbarous.

In this article, I have tried to show that Wole Soyinka's attitude to tradition is unflattering. The setting of all his plays to date is in Africa, but one does not get the impression that he, like many other current African writers, merely sets out to explain the traditions of his people as an end in itself. On the contrary, the sentiments expressed usually

have significance far and wide, although the African environment does lend colour to them. This is why he is able to recognise a sameness of disposition in characters as apparently different as the ancient Helen of Troy, the medieval Madame Tortoise and the modern Rola. This is also why he regards Oba Danlola and Kongi as kindred spirits and finds the same cunning tendency in the Biblical Serpent and the Serpent of the Swamps. Human crimes or foibles are outside time and place and so there is no need specially to upbraid some while extolling others. Only a shallow understanding of Africa or a deliberate (convenient) falsification can produce the kind of lurid generalisation or idealisation some people have indulged in.

This author wants to do away with cant, to expose 'illustrious' ancestors and the stratagems of Messiahs. Today's African may be a little more bizarre than his contemporaries, but he still has the same essence. Thus it is universal human nature that is explored in these plays, only the setting is particularised in time and place. We are confronted with the same problems, the same intensity of feeling and the same conventional solutions or lack of solutions.

COMMENTS

An Additional Comment on Ayi Kwei Armah's *The Beautyful Ones Are Not Yet Born*

Margaret Folarin

As yet, few noteworthy novels on the post-Independence scene in English-speaking West Africa have appeared in print. It is therefore not unreasonable that one should look closely at such works as *A Man of the People, The Interpreters* and *The Beautyful Ones are Not Yet Born*[1] as these indicate some significant lines along which the novel here is probably moving with regard to its themes and its treatment of them.

A retrospective glance will show that the novel written about the time of Independence fell most easily into the medium of a realistic and, at times naturalistic, novel since it was much concerned with the cultivation of the 'African image' through a fairly straight-forward, generally appreciative, exposition of everyday life and culture. The novel about life immediately following Independence fell easily into the critical medium of satire since it was naturally preoccupied, in its disillusionment with the striking failures of political and social life. The shortcomings of the public world can easily be blown up and whipped with satire.

116 But satire can be a limiting, if at times, a most suitable medium, for the literary artist. It can restrict sympathies and close a door against a more profound exploration of the human predicament. It is not unnatural perhaps to find Soyinka writing *The Interpreters* at about the same time as his satirical play *Kongi's Harvest*. There is satire, of course, in *The Interpreters* but the novel is primarily concerned with the emotional experience of creative men who feel restricted by the limitations of the society in which they live. They are forced to stand apart from that society and try to create their own moral and aesthetic values which will allow them to realise their own potential. The passages of satirical comedy in the novel are significantly crossed with highly poetic sections in which the writer experiments with symbolism of a kind which allows him to feel below the surface of life to its roots and springs.

If *The Interpreters* is more explorative and ambitious than *The Beautyful Ones Are Not Yet Born*, the latter novel seems to me almost more revealing of the same processes at work. Once again the writer presents a work of fiction about the undermining effects of corruption, not simply on economic and political, but also spiritual, life. Again the book is concerned with the individual who, demanding deep aesthetic and ethical satisfaction from life, is pushed to live by and unto himself. Again the satire is interspersed with poetic and symbolic passages which allow the writer to explore the situation in depth.

The novel is primarily concerned with two individuals who cannot conform with society, namely the Man and his Teacher. Less energetically rebellious than Soyinka's 'interpreters', the two men feel themselves paralysed by their isolation. They cannot live with others in the corrupt world and, on the other hand, they cannot live without them. The Man returns to society just at the moment when he has escaped from it. The naked Teacher, who has stripped himself of all social ties, still knows that he cannot live fully without love and with the guilt of having rejected his 'loved ones'. In other words, he cannot live fully with hope, for he is a realist, but without hope, without a vision of the birth of a better life in Ghana, he can only vegetate or escape into the life of foreign books and music. Society crushes the spirit of such individuals because it does not allow them to fulfil their relationships with others.

A close look at the development of the novel and its imagery will help reveal the depth and subtlety of the author's vision of this human predicament.

The pivotal image in the book seems to me that of the cave taken from Plato's *Republic*, and the development of the novel can usefully be seen by tracing this recurrent image and its function. It appears in one **117** guise or another on almost every other page and seems to offer a key to much of the novel's meaning. To begin with, by referring the reader to *The Republic*, it can help suggest the topic which is under central consideration in both Plato's work and *The Beautyful Ones Are Not Yet Born* – the question of whether 'the just life' is the right one both in private and public affairs. As in *The Republic* the question is left open until the writer has presented a picture of the state under unjust conditions. The reader is left to draw his own conclusions but by implication Armah, not unnaturally, sides with the honest, if impotent, Man and it is seen that the state will live or die, depending, as in *The Republic*, on the spirit of those who administer its institutions.

Armah makes extensive and intensive use of Plato's image. The Teacher, whose voice is heard in the philosophical chapter 6, is a thoughtful man, who, like Plato's philosopher, turns from the spectacle of his own shadow projected on the wall of the cave and climbs to the cave mouth to look on a vision of the real world illuminated by the sun outside. Like Plato's figure, he has a vision of 'the good', of timeless and universal values such as those of justice, truth, equality and beauty, while those who remain underground continue to be obsessed by the spectacle of the transitory, materialistic and selfish delights of the world. But the Teacher is unlike Plato's philosopher in that he seems unable to return to the cave to illuminate the life of those who live there. If he goes back, not only will people fail initially to respond to what he has to say (the fate awaiting the philosopher who returns to the cave in *The Republic*), but, human nature being what it is, he feels they will never respond, and consequently he sees no point returning to them.

The life of the Man illustrates what happens when honest men return to the cave. The man is more of an 'everyman' than the philosopher. He has married. He has children. He must work for them all day and go back to them at night. Occasionally he too climbs out into the sunlight, but generally he is seen descending into the darkness of the cave which, of course, represents people's experience of life in a corrupt society where values have become cheap and distorted.

The people in the cave do not live in total darkness. They too pursue a light, but it is the light of a Hades, a 'gleam', which appears bright when set in darkness. It is equivalent to the light of the fire which throws the shadows into relief on the wall of Plato's cave and, of course, it is a deceptive light. In *The Beautyful Ones Are Not Yet Born* it is particularly the appeal of material possessions bought corruptly with money and power.

Home is the darkest place for the Man. This is not because his wife
118 and family are more deceived by the 'gleam' than others, but because

the family is affected by the Man's apparent inadequacy; at home he has to face his powerlessness to assist those whose predicament hurts him deeply because he loves them. In short, he has to face what he sees as his own failure. When he descends the office stairs to go home in chapter 3, 'a shadow (rises) menacingly up the bottom wall to meet him, and it is his own.' (p. 40)[1]

At such a moment the Man seems to be a good example of the people in the cave chained down to face shadows. But it is important to notice that the Man is not a typical cave-dweller. He only participates in cave life up to a point. His shadow does not represent desirable pleasures but his own pathetic inadequacy. He sees the shadow as a shadow. He is not deceived about its nature.

Other small facts force the reader to discriminate about the Man's state in the cave. For instance, although when the Man is first encountered in the novel, he is fast asleep as are the other inhabitants of the cave, he is gradually seen to be more awake than those around him. He is, at least, 'a listener'. Others, like the somnambulist cleaner in his office, cannot even hear when they are spoken to. Again, when the Man arrives home (chapter 4) his wife accuses him of being a chichidodo, the bird that eats worms but hates shit, but the accusation is only partly true. Certainly the Man belongs to his wife's world and he participates in the illicit dealings of Koomson in so far as he turns a blind eye to these. He accepts the point that if his wife benefits by contact and contract with the minister and his family, he may too. But the Man does not 'eat' bribes nor does he sign Koomson's papers; nor, in fact, does he appear to desire the luxuries the new rich enjoy though he is sensitive enough to appreciate the sense of power and well-being such things seem to provide.

The Man is lonely but not so isolated as his Teacher. His loneliness is that of someone who belongs to two worlds which oppose each other; his alliance with both prevents him participating in either. After his wife's accusations on this occasion he is too miserable to remain at home and he goes out into the night:

> The night was a dark tunnel so long that out in front and above there never could be any end to it, and to the man walking down it it was plain that the lights here and there illuminated nothing so strongly as they did the endless power of the night, easily, softly calling every sleeping thing into itself. Looking all around him the man saw that he was the only thing that had no way of answering the call of the night. His eyes were hurting in their wakefulness . . . (pp. 54–5)

(The Man's plight here reminds one of that of Plato's philosopher who, **119** going back into the cave after his sojourn in the sunlight, must find it harder to see in the dim light than those accustomed to living in darkness.)

The Man's steps now move towards the residence of his friend, the Teacher, who seems to be aloof from the corruption. The Teacher's words have often raised the Man from his depressions but his thoughts before he reaches his destination allow the reader to see that the Man does not consider escaping from the dark world to live in alienated isolation. The Man is thinking as he goes of another friend:

> 'Rama Krishna. A Ghanaian, but he had taken that far-off name in the reincarnation of his soul after long and tortured flight from everything close and everything known, since all around him showed him the horrible threat of decay. Soul eaten up with thoughts of evergreen things and of an immortality'(p. 55) [he eventually died of consumption and] 'It was whispered . . . that the disease had completely eaten up the frail matter of his lungs, and that where his heart ought to have been there was only a living lot of worms gathered together tightly in the shape of a heart. And so what did the dead rot inside the friend not have to do with his fear of what was decaying outside of himself? And what would such an unnatural flight be worth at all, in the end?' comments the Man. (p. 56)

The Teacher is not a madman. He is not deluded. He knows his life is no better, that probably it is worse, than the Man's. He is awake to the impotency and even decadence of his way of living and in this state he has no comforting words of hope for his friend who has come to visit him.

A chapter is now given to presenting a flashback impression of the wasteland in which the Teacher has lived. The section reduces the tension of the book but it makes points which help extend the meaning of the cave image and the novel generally. It is here particularly that life in the cave is seen in terms of the world of time, change and endless flux. The Teacher conceives this 'turning world' in much the same way as T. S. Eliot, in the sense that he feels time is subject to cyclic change which appears to be drying up at its sources.

The teacher's life began at the end of the colonial era and he describes this period in Ghana to illustrate his first experience of a cycle of life. The period ended, not with a great enlightenment of 'the dark continent' blindly envisaged by the colonialists, but with an era of social injustice, and violence initiated by frustrated soldiers returning from World War II. Even at that time the Teacher tried to escape the confines of the dark world of the cave and seek a 'still point' in the 'turning world', not by ways of intellectual or mystical contemplation but by smoking the drug, wee. Wee, however, is seen as having much the same effect on the smoker as realistic thinking should have on the philosopher. It opens the eyes to reality:

> Wee is not magic. It is just that all through life we protect ourselves in so many ways from so many hurtful truths just by managing to be a little blind here, a bit shortsighted there, and by squinting against the incoming light all the time. That is what the prudent call life. The destructive thing wee does is to lift the blindness and to let you see the whole of your life laid out in front of you. (p. 82)

The Teacher smokes wee with Kofi Billy, the soldier, and Maanan, the prostitute, on the sand by the sea, an environment which inevitably creates images of successive cycles of time. To Kofi Billy, the man of action, who has recently lost a leg in an accident, wee unveils the horror of a future life of vegetation, and he escapes this by committing suicide. To the Teacher and the prostitute Maanan it reveals some of the possibilities which love and beauty offer – the possibilities of union and communion with the human and, to some extent the physical, universe. The Teacher finds he cannot respond adequately to such appeals because, like the warrior, who is faced with the opportunity of making love to a woman on a similar seashore in Armah's short story 'An African Fable', he is oppressed by the feeling that his emotions are ephemeral and therefore ultimately impotent. Later when Maanan falls in love with the new leader the point is taken up again and love and beauty are seen as forces which could move, not only individuals, but society, to climb out of the cave. The new leader is able to inspire men with feeling for each other. What he advocates is virtually an ideal republic where men work as equals for the benefit of each other and not just for themselves. 'The promise,' comments the Teacher, 'was so beautiful. The beauty was in the waking of the powerless.'

It is when power corrupts the beauty of the new leader's ideals that the Teacher refuses to believe in any further dream of a better world. He can only live with his pessimistic vision of inevitably endemic corruption which he feels is a vision of reality. This is why he can only live alone, naked, outside the cave.

The Man listens and hears the Teacher's verdict:

> 'He is not so far in the cave that he cannot hear what is said. But,' he asks, 'What can a person do with things that continue unsatisfied inside? Is their stifled cry not also life?' (p. 100)

The Teacher's philosophy having failed him, he returns home and accepts his family's involvement in the acquisition of Koomson's boat **121** bought out of funds the minister has embezzled. The Man knows his family will gain nothing materially from the venture but those in the cave cannot hear his warning. When the coup comes he helps Koomson evade justice and fly the country on the boat which offers another escape from everything that lies in darkness at home. But the Man, of course, finds that life is more contaminated and foul in its escape route than it was at home, and while such as Koomson can leave country and family, the Man, tied to his domestic commitments and nauseated by the stench on his clothing of the latrine through which he has escaped, plunges off the boat into the sea and its disinfecting salt. But he can only keep his own body clean. He has no faith in the new regime and as he walks home 'very slowly' on this morning after the coup, he can already observe how the new rulers are following exactly in the steps of those they have superseded. He has a vision of Maanan deserted and mad on the sand by the sea. Once again beauty, which might have led men out of the cave, has been adulterated. It has been conceived, perhaps, but never born.

The conclusion to be drawn from such a glance at the novel would seem to be that human nature will always be like this. Man will always fail woman. Power will always corrupt. Spiritual and ethical values will be for ever cheapened by the ways of the world, and therefore on the human, political and economic level there is no exit from life in the cave as it has been presented in the novel.

If this were all, Armah's book might seem too pessimistic and superficial. It would leave one with an unnecessary sense of individual and social impotence. The image of the cave would simply serve to throw into relief the absurdity of idealism like that of Plato and others who feel reform is worth working for and that justice and honesty pay in public and private life. But when one looks at other incidents and images in the novel it will be found, I think, that Plato's sentiments on the rightness of 'the just life' are not mocked but reinforced by Armah's work and that the cave image finally serves as a nucleus which holds together these positive meanings.

It is important to notice first of all that the author's vision is not necessarily the same as that of the Man or the Teacher and that many of their conclusions are not, in fact, conclusive. One is forced to feel this way, I think, because many of the images bristle with almost Heraclitean paradox and consequently reveal a deep and discriminating understanding of human values and predicaments. The final values which emerge from the book seem to me not unpositive. The novel is certainly not simply a censorious gesture against a corrupt society.

122 It is helpful now to look more carefully at the Maanan passages for although not Armah's most successful, they cast light on the complex value of life as it is presented in the book. When the Teacher is smoking wee with Maanan on the beach and is suddenly made conscious of the beauty of womankind (Maanan bears the face and form of ages of women), he becomes aware at the same time of mankind's inability to 'make good' such beauty. His vision is therefore also of the suffering of womankind.[2] This realisation is at one point presented through an image: the Teacher reaches out 'a searching hand' seemingly towards Maanan 'but in the end' he only holds 'a handful of fine, beautiful sand, and the beauty of the sand' takes away his gaze from 'the troubled beauty of the woman beside' him. (p. 85).

> I could not help it, [he continues] 'As the moist sand dripped through my weakened fingers and joined the shore. Like an animal I knelt down and stretched out my hand to wash the sand away with the farthest coming water of the waves, and then suddenly I felt like taking the salt water into my mouth. It was not only salt I tasted, but a hundred other strong things in the water, and I cleansed my mouth with it and spat it out slowly and did it all again. Something that did not want to die made me touch Maanan softly on the side of her mouth. For a long time my hand rested there and I looked at her and I was lost in despair.' (p. 86)

The image of salt and the image of the sea are recurrent in the novel. Like many other images they represent the cycle of life. Salt, like the sea, is the destroyer but it is also the preserver of living things, an instrument of decay and of cleansing. Salt water contains traces of life in its beginnings and its endings. What the sand and sea eat out of the earth they use to recreate more land. Salt water, therefore, has the taste of the 'strong things' it has destroyed. Salt makes life appetising; life seems valuable when it has suffered a 'sea change'. The sea is thus cleansing and refreshing to the Teacher it makes him want to live and love so that he again reaches out and touches, if briefly, the woman he feels for. He 'despairs' surely because, like Marlowe's Faustus, he has tasted the joys of Heaven and feels they can never be his.

But the cleansing image of the salt stands, whatever the Teacher's personal feelings of inadequacy. It shows that the renewal of life can come through hard experience and the death and disintegration of what is corrupt. This interpretation is reinforced if the image is compared with others in the novel, for instance with those of the polish on the banisters and the gleaming white keep-your-city-clean cans in chapter 1. Both these images reflect the efforts of those who follow 'the gleam' to brighten and refresh their lives. As such people are deceived or hypocritical about the nature of cleanness; they simply resort to putting **123** polish over the dirt. The Komsoons' life, for instance, acquires such a gleaming surface that the Man's wife is taken in by it and thinks the life of the minister's wife, the glittering Estella, 'is clean'. Later, of course, when Koomson's life goes up in smoke, or rather fumes, she finds how inwardly it stinks. (I am continually reminded in this book of two of the *Fragments* of Heraclitus: 'If all existing things were smoke, it is by smell that we would distinguish them,' and 'In Hades souls perceive by smelling.'[3])

There are other paradoxical images in the book like those of sea, salt and cleanness. Those of darkness and light and those of fresh water as they appear in certain passages in chapter 3 will, I hope, serve adequately to reinforce my points.

The time is midday. Even those in the dim interior of the railway offices where the Man works know that the sun is up outside because of the 'stewy atmosphere' within. It is Passion Week:

'At a time like this, when the month was so far gone and all there was was the half-life of Passion Week, lunchtime was not a time to refresh oneself.'

The passage has a metaphorical as well as a literal meaning for it continues by commenting that people have:

seen enough of something in their own lives and in the lives around them to convince them of the final futility of efforts to break the mean monthly cycle of debt and borrowing, borrowing and debt. Nothing was left beyond the necessity of digging oneself deeper and deeper into holes in which there could never be anything like life . . . Even the efforts one made not to join [these underground dwellers it is felt] may be in the end . . . resulted only in another, more frustrating kind of death. (p. 25)

Nevertheless the Man does try to refresh himself – if not physically, at least, spiritually. He skips the lunch he cannot really afford and walks out into the sunlight along the railway line away from the crowds:

The sourness that had been gathering in his mouth went imperceptibly away until quite suddenly all he was aware of was the exceedingly sharp clarity of vision and the clean taste that comes with the successful defiance of hunger . . . Nothing oppressed him as he walked along now, and even the slight giddiness accompanying the clarity of his starved vision was buried way beneath the unaccustomed happy lightness. (p. 26)

As so often in this novel the images of happiness are adulterated by something unpleasant just as those of misery are mollified by something positive associated with them. One notices here, for instance, that it is not the Man's stomach, but his vision in the sunlight which is 'starved'. He is freed from the physical and mundane pressures of life (some might say his vision has something of the spiritual and mystical about it), but there is also the implication here that, once again, life outside the cave is empty.

The impression is reinforced a little later when the man crosses a bridge where a fallen cement block creates a dam in a sluggish stream. Behind the dam:

> all the filth seemed to have got caught for a hanging moment, so that the water escaping through a gap made the little dam and the far side of the ditch had a cleanness which had nothing to do with the thing it came out from. Even from the small height of the dam, the water hit the bottom of the ditch with sufficient force to eat away the soft soil down to the harder stuff beneath, exposing a bottom of smooth pebbles with the clear water now flowing over it. How long-lasting the clearness? Far out, toward the mouth of the small stream and the sea, he could see the water already aging into the mud of its beginnings. He drew back his gaze and was satisfied with the clearness before the inevitable muddying. It was the satisfaction of a quiet attraction, not at all like the ambiguous disturbing tumult within awakened by the gleam. And yet here undoubtedly was something close enough to the gleam, this clearness, this beautiful freedom from dirt. Somehow, there seemed to be a purity and a peace here which the gleam could never bring. (p. 27)

The image of the clear water in this passage surely suggests that clean, fresh experiences can be discovered even amongst the filthiest ones of life. Satisfaction can be found even in the cave.

The point, however, may be taken further. The image could suggest that clear vision and understanding belong only to those who have not evaded the dark facts about life. This idea is made explicit I think by a later image of fresh water. In chapter 6 the Teacher is describing a visit he made as a child to the European residential area of his town. The Europeans there lived on the hills outside the town where the water was still fresh before its contact with the African township below. To the Teacher the water seemed like 'unused water, or like water used by ghosts without flesh.' (p. 78). Ghosts is a word Armah seems to attach to those who live aloof from 'the common man'. (Even the Teacher calls himself a ghost because he lives apart from his 'loved ones'.)

These images, then, surely give another dimension to the author's vision of life in the cave. The cave is a dark place certainly, but there is **125** also the suggestion that one must have some experience of it before one can acquire the knowledge that will give life full meaning. Life in the cave forms virtually the experience of evil that brings forth good. Life is not to be found simply in Eden.

The point may be confirmed I think by turning to Armah's essay on 'African Socialism: utopian or scientific'[4] which appeared in *Presence Africaine* a year before the publication of *The Beautyful Ones Are Not Yet Born*. In this article Armah seems to be arguing for a socialism which is neither 'utopian' (back to Eden) or 'scientific' in the sense he feels Nkrumah falsely interpreted the 'scientific' ideas of the Marxists. When he wrote the article Armah obviously felt that the period of bogus African socialism would end with the disappearance of the immediate post-Independence leaders, who would die out because they belonged to 'a specific class' which was 'transitional'. He prophesied the birth of two alternative forms of rule which would supersede 'African Socialism' as he felt it then existed. These would be either:

> a backward, reactionary return to colonial patterns or a progressive revolution . . . The first, the backward retrenchment, is so far the only logical step for which colonial and Post-Independence experiences have been preparing the African people. The other alternative, a revolutionary restructuring of lines of authority, has only academic interest at this point. Classes exist in Africa. Furthermore, there are spectacular differences in standards of living and access to privileges and services provided through the use of common wealth of the states. So the dynamite is there. What is so far lacking is a widespread consciousness of connections between socio-economic inequalities and the structures of the social order. This consciousness cannot be taught or learnt in hot-house institutions like so much Greek or Mathematics. It has to grow out of the visible, audible and sensible facts of life in each society, especially when these socities have hordes of poor people and yet enjoy politico-economic systems that encourage the growth of a propertied, prosperous minority. When this happens the naturally growing consciousness of people may be compared to a fuse. And it is only then that it makes sense for the revolutionary agitator to talk of striking a spark.

Whatever one may think of this passage, two points are clear. In the first place it is obvious that Armah feels social change must be brought about by the 'poor people', not by those who subjugate them nor those with aloof academic interests in the social scene. The knowledge which will bring people up from their underground environment must 'grow out of the visible, audible and sensible facts of life in each society'. In the second place it is clear that Armah does not share the Teacher's pessimism, feeling that new and old governments and authorities will be everlastingly identical. Armah's article here claims that 'the dynamite' that will explode on the eve of real revolution 'already exists' and that it is only a question of time before the spark is put to it. On the social and political level, at least, he feels there will be revolutionary change.

A comparison of the first and last chapters will, I hope, finally summarise my points. My main point is this: although the situation seems outwardly the same at the beginning and end of *The Beautyful Ones Are Not Yet Born* (life continues corruptly in the public world despite the coup, and the Man appears to be returning to the same situation at home and at work) the Man's human predicament has been redefined.

In the first chapter he was found asleep on a 'dark dawn'; in the last, after his cleansing plunge into the sea and his sleep on the sand, he wakes in brilliant morning sunlight. True, the first person he sees is Maanan, in some ways the most potential force in the novel, and Maanan is mad. Her love for the new leader has come to nothing and like the Teacher earlier she lets the sand slip through her fingers. However, she seems to be sifting it in search for what she has lost, presumably her vision of love and beauty, but she cannot find this because they have mixed it all with so many other things'. Her vision has been adulterated by the worldly ambitions of the man she loved. It is also true that this Maanan passage reminds one of the teacher's understanding of life as recorded by the man in his role as 'listener'.

> What a painful kind of understanding . . . words that mix the beauty with the ugliness, words making the darkness twin with the light, and in the end he says what he now believes, that in the end there is the one remaining truth. (p. 92)

The remaining truth from the teacher's point of view would seem to be that life is without hope – without the hope that people in the cave will ever be undeceived about the nature of 'the gleam' and walk out into the radiance of the sun. But, as I hope to have shown, the experience presented in the novel does not necessarily point to such a straight conclusion. Given the situation in the novel there is probably more life inside the cave than there is outside. On this last occasion when Maanan is seen in the final chapter, she finally walks away from the sun towards the distant town. She does so surely, like the Man, not because she is unaware, even in her madness, of the realities of life but because she is aware of them. As she goes her shadow in front of her is seen colouring, not darkening, the sand.

The bus in the last chapter is deceptively bright and new. Morally speaking it is as decrepit as the rattletrap which shudders its way over the first pages of the book. Its driver is more sophisticated in his corrupt **127** little dealings than the conductor of the first vehicle. But the new bus has a motto which is not one of necessary despair. It does not suggest that 'the beautyful ones' can never be born. The flower which presumably illustrates the caption is 'very beautiful' (p. 214) unlike the pasted brick 'flower pattern' on the Railway and Harbour Administration Block in chapter 1. Finally when the image of the beautiful flower design on the bus disappears it is replaced by a 'melodious note'. (p. 215)

The Man follows the bus through the police check-point and down a hill. At the bottom there is the familiar image of a latrine and flying around it is a bird, the chichidodo. Its song is 'strangely happy'. (p. 215) The comment is, of course, ambiguous. It may be ironic, but it may also mean that there is life and even genuine happiness to be had even where society is rotten and corrupt.

The Man goes on – 'back to Oyo' (his wife) and 'the eyes of the children after six o'clock, the office and everyday, and above all the never-ending knowledge that his aching emptiness would be all that the remainder of his own life could offer him'. (p. 215) But again, it should be remembered that Oyo has now learnt a certain, if limited, respect for her husband's 'absurd' honesty, and at the end of the previous chapter it is said that the Man's loneliness gives him 'a vague freedom', and that it is 'untroubled'. (p. 210) It is untroubled, if aching, presumably because since Koomson let the Man's wife down over the boat deal, the Man's line of action and inaction, his life of honest integrity, has proved at least better than the life of those who involve themselves in the corruption itself.

Armah's pessimism may be even distasteful to some readers, but it does not seem to me a pessimism which need limit the vision of *The Beautyful Ones Are Not Yet Born*, for Armah seems to be very aware of the positive values of life and the book does not pour scorn on these or those who work for them. 'Beauty' as it is conceived in the novel can exist and may be born.

The novel seems to me a bold and cleansing one. It begins with a refusal to accept any sentimental facts about human nature or the social scene. It accepts life as it may be observed at its very worst and then still unravels, if in a rather humourless way, much of the value of human existence.

NOTES

1. *The Beautyful Ones Are Not Yet Born* published by Houghton Mifflin, Boston, 1969, and Heinemann, London, 1969.
2. Also perhaps of Africa. The figure of Maanan is so like that of the woman who represents Africa in Armah's *African Fable* it is hard not to see Maanan too as such a symbol.
3. *Heraclitus* by Philip Wheelwright (Princeton, 1959), p. 59. (*Fragments* 58 and 59.)
4. 'African Socialism: utopian or scientific,' *Présence Africaine*, No. 64, 1967, pp. 6–30.

Camara Laye's
The African Child
A Reply

David Carroll

The African Child is not a major work of fiction, but it is a much better novel than Paul Edwards and Kenneth Ramchand suggest in their recent attack, 'Camara Laye: An African Sentimentalist', in *African Literature Today*, No. 4. While agreeing with some of their later comments on the presentation of life in Conakry, I was surprised by the nature of their criticism of Laye's striking picture of childhood. I would suggest they have been misled into imposing on the novel far too naïve a structure and then been disappointed when the work failed to conform to it. For them the organisation of *The African Child* is extremely simple. The novel consists of two parts: the first eight chapters portraying the hero's childhood 'add up to an orderly picture of coherent traditional life and community'; the last four describe his growing 'detachment from his sustaining context of African village life' as he moves to Conakry and finally to Paris. Since the narrator is saddened by the change from the first to the second part of the novel, they conclude that *The African Child* is committed to an anti-colonial line on the level of cultural polemics. Having stated their thesis, they become impatient when certain episodes and ideas blur its clear and simple outline. If the first part of **129** the novel is supposed to present the 'picture of an ideally happy, courteous and well-adjusted society', they ask, why do all kinds of nasty things like violence, ambition, and bullying occur there? In other words, why doesn't the author write his novel in as consistently tendentious a way as they say he ought to have done? One answer is that perhaps it is the thesis rather than the novel which is at fault.

The basic pattern of *The African Child* is to be found not in cultural polemics but in much more traditional forms. The first memory of the narrator, on the first page of the novel, is of a moment of discovery. Within the familiar sound of his parents' voices, the young child has begun to play his innocent game with the snake. Just before it buries its fangs into his hand, the child is snatched away by one of his father's apprentices and soundly slapped by his hysterical mother. His sudden arrival in this fallen world of sin and suffering leads him, a few pages later, to ask the traditional questions about the nature of good and evil. 'There were good spirits, and there were evil ones; and more evil than good ones, it seemed to me. And how was I to know that this snake was harmless? It looked the same as any other snake . . .' (*The African Child*, trans. James Kirkup, Fontana Books, 1955, p. 16). From this point, the child is self-conscious and frequently perplexed by the world in which he finds himself, he never regains the security and complete happiness of the first two paragraphs of the novel. He has embarked on what he calls later 'the highway of life, the one we set foot on when we are born, and which is only the highway of our momentary exile'. (p. 150) Next, he begins to discover that his world is divided between his parents who represent different values, and this in turn brings the problem of choice, the difficulty of decision, and the inevitable regret. This opening sequence, finely observed and unobtrusively shaped, suggests the traditional and universal pattern which gives meaning to this fictional autobiography. If this is polemic, it is directed against the fallen world of time which has replaced the Garden of Eden.

The narrator's father and mother provide the alternative values upon which the novel is constructed and which, in the course of his childhood, become increasingly divergent. Again, the contrast follows traditional lines. The father, a worker in metal in Kouroussa, the small town where the child grows up, is an important figure in the community and the chief smith in the five cantons. As artificer, he displays the customary masculine skills of imposing order and form upon inert matter, and from the exercise of his magical and creative powers he emerges as a commanding figure. In the impressive account of the making of the gold trinket – sensitively analysed by Edwards and Ramchand – he takes the precious metal which has been coaxed out of the mud of the river and by his skill and invocations he slowly and ritualistically transforms it into a thing of beauty. It is noticeable that as the process moves to its climax and the elements of gold, fire, and air are controlled and combined, the smith becomes more and more dominant as the chief actor to whom all the other characters – the praise-singer, the apprentices, the owner of the gold – are subordinate. Then comes the celebrated chant of the douga and he alone dances:

> At the first notes of the douga, my father would rise and utter a cry in which happiness and triumph were equally mingled; and brandishing in his right hand the hammer that was the symbol of his profession, and in his left a ram's horn filled with magic substances, he would dance the glorious dance. (p. 31)

The father has reached this position of pre-eminence through his own efforts as we learn later in the novel when he tells his son of his wretched childhood as an orphan and his exploitation by his uncles. 'I always had to keep my own counsel and work hard to make a name for myself'. (p. 117) So, although he represents important traditional skills in the community, he has achieved his unique position there by means of ambition and individual striving and these are the values he is the exponent of in the novel. His final words of advice as his son leaves for Conakry are: 'Seize your opportunity. And make me proud of you. I ask no more of you.' (p. 117) And this, of course, is the advice the narrator takes; it leads him from Kouroussa, to Conakry, and finally to Paris. In Conakry, the father's guiding role is assumed by his brother Mamadou, who has become managing director of a French firm and lives in a European-style house. This is the road of ambition mapped out for the African child and he follows it, surpassing his uncle and moving to the metropolitan centre. In retrospect, the narrator does not need to dwell on the nature of these hopes and ambitions since they are being acted out for the reader; instead, he returns repeatedly and nostalgically to the alternative he did not choose, the values represented by his mother. This is the genuine sadness of the novel, and this is why the opening verses are addressed to her: 'Black woman, woman of Africa, O my mother, I am thinking of you . . .'

She is the other dominant personality of the novel. As the first two chapters, which have been devoted to the father, end with his celebrated dance, the narrative switches abruptly to the mother angrily pounding millet in the yard. She disapproves of the father endangering his eyesight and she tells her son that he would be better off playing outside instead of breathing the dust and smoke of the workshop. But the real reason she seeks to undercut her husband's triumph seems to be **131** the realisation that fame and success of this kind will inevitably lead her son away from the home, and she is opposed to this for her values are maternal, traditional, and authoritarian. The difference should not be exaggerated, but it is clear that she rules the domestic life of the family and the apprentices by strict principles of order which she enforces zealously. Her values, as the opening verses imply, lead the child, not to France, but back to the country, to her ancestral village of Tindican: 'Woman of the fields, woman of the rivers, woman of the great river-banks. O you my mother, I am thinking of you . . .'

Tindican represents 'the life of the country-side and the fields' (p. 33) with which Kouroussa has lost contact, and which the child comes to understand on his regular visits there to his maternal uncles and grandmother. After the latter has given him his ritual bath to wash off the dust of his journey from Kouroussa, he is ready to join the children in the fields and play tentatively with the animals. Although he remains the town-dweller in the country, he is strongly influenced by this way of life which embodies the maternal qualities of natural growth and creativity. His grandmother's hut is very similar to his mother's except for one thing, the maize hanging from the roof which 'might have served as a rustic calendar, for as the harvest-time came round again, their number would decrease, until finally there would be none left'. (p. 39) Here, life waits patiently upon the weather, the seasons, and the spirits of the soil, but, it should be added, Tindican is no pastoral dream-world for the men toil and sweat in the fields. Their work, however, affects them differently from his father's creative performances. The scene which demonstrates this most vividly is the harvesting of the rice, and this is contrasted implicitly with the set-piece at the forge. Here in the fields too there is effort, and creation, and song, but they are differently ordered. The farmers work together, in unison, and his uncle Lansana is careful not to appear to be reaping faster than his colleagues. As the tempo increases, the workers lose the sense of their separateness, expressing their oneness by means of song: 'they were singing in chorus, and reaping in unison: their voices and their gestures were all harmonious, and in harmony; they were one! – united by the same task, united by the same song'. (p. 51) Attendant upon the creative processes of nature, they become rapt in an 'inner dream', aware not of themselves as creators but only of 'the mute mystery of things'. (p. 43) Tindican clearly leads away from ambition and pre-eminence, away from the individual's desire to control the elements and distinguish himself in the community. This is the life Lansana has chosen, leading his brothers away from 'the paternal forge'.

Paul Edwards and Kenneth Ramchand notice this difference of emphasis – 'The rice harvest episode posits a sense of community, but not in the same way as the goldsmith's shop sequence, and without comprehending as many different individuals' – but they see this as a weakness, a falling off, a further sign of 'a disguised polemic intention'. They feel that they are required to contrast happy peasant life with 'the mechanised and sterile civilisation' of Europe. Surely this is their own extrapolation. The significant contrast, the one they noticed briefly and dismissed, is the far more specific one between Kouroussa and Tindican, between the values of the father and those of the mother. The child chooses the former and these lead him eventually to Europe and away from both parents, but Europe remains a subordinate element in the pattern of choices which is being established during these early days of childhood. The contrast is not overstressed, but, as the child pays his frequent visits to his mother's family and then returns to Kouroussa, he watches carefully, he asks questions, and the two worlds become juxtaposed in his mind. Each gains in meaning and definition by the contrast.

The central part of the novel describes the boy's education at Kouroussa and again we see his parents reacting in their characteristic ways. The mother at first opposes each new stage of his education, both in the traditional system and the new, for she is fighting the inevitability of her son growing up and leaving home. But on each occasion she comes to accept its necessity and then she lends her support; and it is clear that the rituals of initiation are carefully contrived to bring about this disengagement as painlessly as possible. As her influence wanes during this process, the father becomes more dominant, encouraging his son in his education and his ambition. But he does not accept his son's schooling uncritically. And it is in the perspective of what he wishes his son to become that the traditional initiation and the system of the French school are carefully compared. This is another subordinate contrast within the larger scheme of the novel which is obscured by the uniform stereotype of childhood imposed by Edwards and Ramchand.

In his characteristic way, the author simply juxtaposes the two kinds of education. At the French school, the headmaster has handed his power over to the older boys who tyrannise over the younger ones in a cruel and arbitrary way. The central episode of this tyranny, the whipping of the younger boys as they are forced to clear the leaves from the school-yard, becomes a mockery of the earlier happy harvest scene at Tindican. 'So at an order from the older boys we would all line up like peasants about to reap or glean a field, and we would set to work like members of a chain-gang.' (p. 69) They can only escape a beating by **133** bribing the senior boys with the food they have taken for their midday meal. For some time they keep their treatment secret, but then one child resists, a parent takes action, and the narrator's father attacks the headmaster who is finally dismissed. It is significant that the father intervenes because his son is being reduced to a state of submissiveness and slavery, 'completely at variance', says the narrator, 'with our passion for independence and equality', qualities which the traditional rites have begun to develop in the boys.

Many of the same elements reappear in the rite of Kondén Diara which is described in the next chapter. An age-group of uncircumcised boys is handed over to their elders who lead them off into the bush and then order them to kneel and cover their eyes in preparation for their ordeal. 'Woe to him who would have the audacity to disobey! He would be cruelly whipped.' (p. 84) After their courage has been fully tested by the terrifying roaring of the lions, their education is undertaken by the older boys: 'all night long they will teach us the songs of the uncircumcised; and we must remain quite still, repeating the words after them, singing the melody after them; there we sit, as if we were in school again, attentive, very attentive, and very obedient.' (p. 86) The elements of the earlier episodes have been re-ordered to make the contrast quite clear. Power is here being used ritualistically and responsibly: 'it is a test, a training in hardhip, a rite' (p. 92). The boys are both tested and sustained by the rite of Kondén Diara which takes its place in the larger pattern of initiation which leads to circumcision and maturity. And the contrast with the school is underlined when the child later discovers that the roaring lions were simulated: authority, fear, and secrecy are all being carefully manipulated in the process of initiation. Many of these traditional methods remain for the narrator simply unexplained fragments in the memory because his formal schooling is slowly but surely taking precedence.

The last four chapters of The African Child describe the boy's life after he has left home and is pursuing his studies in Conakry. His departure is an important turning-point in the novel but not the complete break as it is represented by Edwards and Ramchand. I would suggest that the structure of values defined earlier persists in various forms to the very end. For example, whenever the youth pays one of his frequent visits home, his parents continue to exert their influence; when, on the other hand, he is in Conakry, his father's role is carried out by his uncle Mamadou, while Marie, whose love is 'one last and fragile moment of his youth' (p. 137), represents in her mistrust of the sea and the unknown the same kind of conservatism as his mother.

134   The boy is trying to become an independent agent but he finds he still needs the support of both parents. He is sustained and encouraged by his father's hopes which he continues to fulfil, but at the same time he is unwilling to sever finally his maternal ties. His continuing dependence upon the home is indicated by his illness in Conakry and, more melodramatically, by the death of his friend Check; ambition, it is suggested, can exact a heavy price which may be mitigated neither by the medicine-man of the community which is being left behind nor by the white doctor of the society aspired to. It must be acknowledged that frequently there is, as Edwards and Ramchand say, a thinness in the writing of these final chapters. As soon as the boy is separated from the vivid milieu of his childhood he becomes insubstantial as a centre of vision from which to describe life in Conakry. From being the passive recipient of the influences of his parents and the community, he is seeking to become an agent and his indeterminateness is a symptom of this difficult transition.

Finally, it should be added, the author hints at a more general frame of values behind the boy's relationship with his parents. It would be pretentious to call this framework philosophical for it is sketched in lightly and unobtrusively, but it does complete the pattern which has controlled the novel from the beginning. It becomes clear, in these final chapters, that each parent is committed to a particular view of destiny and that the boy, though overtly guided by his father, is conditioned by both of these views. The father's idea is stated most explicitly at the end of the novel when he hears of his son's chance to go to Paris: 'Each one follows his own destiny, my son. Men can do nothing to change it. This opportunity is within your reach: you must seize it.' (p. 153) Here, there is both predestination and free-will, but the stress is upon character as destiny and the duty of the individual to make sure that this destiny is allowed to unfold freely. The mother's view is less explicit but it is clear from her actions that she sees destiny primarily as the outside forces which control the individual. These forces need to be placated, and they may be modified by means of magic potions brought from Moslem holy places and by carefully consulting the marabout. The different emphasis each parent gives leads back, of course, to the forge and the farm, and to the role of the individual in those different worlds. Their joint influence on the mind of the youth is most clearly seen when he is about to take the final examinations in Conakry which will send him to Europe. He is relying ambitiously on his own abilities, but he takes a precaution:

I was absolutely determined to pass my examination. I had studied hard for three years; I had never forgotten the promise I had made to my father, nor yet the one I had made to myself . . . Nevertheless, I **135** wrote to ask my mother to go and see the marabouts and obtain their help. Should I infer from this that I was particularly superstitious at this time? I do not think so. I simply believed that nothing could be obtained without the help of God, and that if the will of God is something preordained, nevertheless our actions, though just as unforeseen, have their influence on that will. (p. 140)

Together, the support of both parents enables him to succeed and thus to leave Africa, a move which his father has accepted with resignation from the beginning but which his mother resists in one final outburst as she again angrily pounds the millet, before she too accepts the inevitable. In their different ways, they have both come to feel that 'the wheels of destiny' (p. 156) are working out their son's future.

REVIEWS

Sympathy and Art:
Novels and Short Stories

Donald Carter

Dying in the Sun, Peter K. Palangyo, Heinemann, 1968.
God's Bits of Wood, Sembene Ousmane, translated by Francis Price, Heinemann, 1970. (A reissue of the Doubleday, New York, edition of 1962.)
Because of Women, Mbella Sonne Dipoko, Heinemann, 1968.
Chief the Honourable Minister, T. M. Aluko, Heinemann, 1970.
Fixions, Taban lo Liyong, Heinemann, 1970, and Praeger, 1971.

I am charged in this issue of *African Literature Today* to look at a batch of novels and short pieces of fiction. The reviewer who aspires to criticism, the critic who fears to fall into cliché, seeks in each case some rubric under which in the interests of a presumed art of literature he can bring his offerings, his current specimens. I am proposing here to try out (hence my title) 'Sympathy and Art' as, in some peculiar sense, to be explored, dispositions opposed to each other. There is clearly, to begin with, in the idea of *this* opposition, an element of the preposterous. How without sympathy may one have art? The question applies quite generally but we can plead with at least the greatest appearance of circumspection where the novel is concerned – concerned as the novel nakedly is with people in their ordinary inter-actions and daily dilemmas. The large tragic scale, the prince, the man **137** removed from ordinary destinies, these do not in general figure in the novel, but in the more concentrated drama. In the novel there is an immediacy of concern with the immediate object: with man not especially resolved into one category or another. Perhaps the definitional air of this begs questions and skirts controversy – still the point is painless to take, the art of the novel could scarcely subsist without on the novelist's part unqualified sympathy, without a warranty of humane feeling that, additions and subtractions endlessly made, still is a good round figure left.

But art we are told belongs to civilisation. In what sense? How lies the artist's debt? We may consider cases demanding, especially demanding, of sympathy. There are novelists whom history or circumstance puts in the way of treating suffering, which is to say conspicuous or out of the way suffering, something differentiated from this condition as the common lot. The position I wish to enunciate is a simple one: that the novelist must himself be to a degree removed from or free from this suffering, that this is the crucial part of what civilisation means for him, and for his readers. Tolstoy deals with peasant suffering but in his direct experience does not have part in it. Now the point about the suffering is that it is – in my sense – *gross*; it is unrelieved; it is unlike in this sense that of Anna Karenina, which is as near to his own experience as Tolstoy came and which because it is relieved may be shaped, may be escaped from into consideration and reflection.

To come abruptly to the point: the African novelist frequently does deal with conspicuous suffering. To put the matter less contentiously his people are closer to the edge of experience. He must exercise sympathy before he can exercise art. Ntanya in Mr Palangyo's novel *Dying in the Sun*, is ill-favoured by nature; born ugly:

He wept that he was ever born,
And he had reasons.

Born of a father quite decidedly ill-favoured and unlovable by nature, having no better luck than willy-nilly to find his bride as she leaves a whore-house, Ntanya still is not shown placed, as his village existence goes, in an out of the way purgatory. You see as you take up the slack of circumstances in the story that Ntanya is not out of the common lot. In the village, in any African village, this lot may be hard, decidedly so. Note that the energetic impulse our thesis decrees is that of sympathy, and that sympathy is in its common meaning taken to be with suffering, though it would be absurd to suppose it withdrawn the moment there was joy or happiness. And I am far from saying that life in traditional

Africa lacks, or lacked, joyousness. Sometimes it is hard to imagine that the total in evidence could be made up elsewhere. But it is and must always have been insecure, close to precipitation into suffering.

The detachment or 'distance' from his subject-matter which is essential to the novelist as artist has been got in the present instance by an education in a language not even belonging to the continent of Africa: in English or French for example; this increases the difficulty, for the African writer, of rendering his experience – as this is the experience of his characters – into 'art'. The difficulty is got over, where seriously engaged, by a paradox: by exercising sympathy; by feeling directly 'sympathetic' the writer is more likely to produce results than by 'going for' art in the sense of literary effect. (And of course this latter fine thing lies, in English and French, everywhere in wait to ambush the aspirant writer.) Mr Palangyo, writing very close to his material, himself not disengaged from his characters, not ironical, not cushioned or otherwise removed from them by class or cultural distance and without benefit, it may without offence be said, of genius (a circumstance which alters cases), would scarcely seem able to avoid an occasional sense of literary jolt and jar. Ntanya in his novel is notwithstanding brought wonderfully through. Few novels can have brought so refractory a character into the final dignity of happiness, of a simple but most prescribable sort – namely marriage and a child – with the book closing on this secure note almost, to the reader's admiration, before it had properly opened on one of, as it had seemed, irrecoverable anguish.

Less successful, the theme and the thing attempted being less tractable to success, is a novel translated from the French, named agreeably *God's Bits of Wood*, and again concerned with, strictly in M. Fanon's sense, the 'wretched of the earth' – the striking railway workers on the Dakar–Niger line, the date being 1947–8 and the villains being the French. The format is that of prose epic – an epic of holding out, of incidental suffering and deprivation, of long endurance insecurely sustained by hope, of an ordeal of French hypocrisy, the rather desperate failure of scruple and moral toe-hold of the late colonists. Amongst the press of events otherwise not too coherent, there is an epic march of women, of which the full catalogue of cruel incident is ferociously detailed for us – but of all of it the shape in the end is that of History, always at best a stand-in Muse. A certain dullness, the weariness of recorded cruel fact infects the narrative. There is the most absolute sympathy. There is determination that the entire large unjust event shall get irremoveably on record. There is a novelistic dexterity in handling a large cast of characters differentiated by little more than that they 'took part'. Here and there are fine vignettes, grateful secretions of **139** true fiction: one thinks for example of (amongst others) the description of 'Hadrame' the Moor's shop, or of the compound in Dakar of Houdia M'Baye. Generally these are a matter of what in 'straight' fiction would be called 'setting' – African settings for which, as often as not entirely squalid in the physical sense, with a terrible rudimentariness of domestic arrangement, the author has a caustically realistic eye, but with this leading him into, rather than away from, participation and compassion. But one cannot expect a true art of fiction to issue. It is still a valuable and interesting book.

Now Mbella Sonne Dipoko's *Because of Women* – in my view you must write with considerable spirit to justify such a title: it has indications of partiality. Women certainly belong in the scheme of things but are not except to the jocosely or perhaps sullenly minded, specially favoured there. There are problems if the novelist ceases to write with God's eye, a sin he is expected to commit, and takes up some brief or other. '*Because of Women* is a study in pleasure and change. The story of a womaniser who dreams of founding a large family. The novel tries to show the deep joy there is in women.' Thus the author. There is I think in this conspectus some uncertainty of aim, and this uncertainty unsettles the book. The one thing in Ngoso is, inevitably, at variance with the other: womanising is, after all, rather a different thing from founding a large family, and though with the aid of the institution of polygamy the one may be made to approximate to the other in result, this consummation is not in fact arranged by the author. There is nothing sociologically in the way of it; merely a certain incongruity, which the characters seem to feel. Now to a finally enfeebling extent Mr Dipoko resorts, in 'trying to show the deep joy there is in women' to more or less set-piece descriptions of the sexual act. Just because Ngoso is a womaniser, and the note is indicated that women are splendid anyway, these descriptions come in rather randomly, opportunity being mistaken, as one might say, for opportuneness. The narrative is apt to straggle and be diffuse – the unit of narrative construction tending apparently to be Ngoso's day and what it might bring. Characteristically perhaps in a womaniser he suffers ennui: this is contagious for the reader. I shall propose a want of 'sympathy': of an adequately felt engagement that is either with the normal sort of hero, *homme* perhaps *moyen sensuel*, or, this being rejected, with the errant, the more or less picaresque character. So Ngoso, womanising, might have been taken up more or less *con brio*, sardonically, satirically, bravely, or on some other distinct plane, in any case with intent to present. Instead there is a feel of embarrassment about the story, as who should **140** (unknown to himself) be preferring to tell a plain, more or less moral, tale, and then find one of the characters defect. The intent is professed, yes, but in words that confess an uncertainty. Why for instance must Ngosi die? Characters in novels (as within the ethos of witchcraft) do not die of natural causes, and there appears here no sufficient reason why the man should be killed off with a fever, other, one is forced to suspect, than the convention-pressures of the moral tale.

Rather than a novelist Mbella Sonne Dipoko appears to me to be a writer; and I may say, not having much enjoyed carping, that he reads like one, being able well to evoke a scene, and giving me much pleasure of curiosity to visit his country.

I wonder whether in *Chief the Honourable Minister* Mr Aluko is being either writer or novelist, as distinct let us say from indignant Nigerian citizen, putting what is at least a fully-tempered literacy, as it were a citizen's side-arm, to the castigation of the (post-Independence) times. Very gratifying to his fellow-citizens, to all friends of Africa, must be this civic clear-sightedness, these sharp cuffs administered to abuse. It may be guessed from the title that we have to do with satire. Yet to confound my thesis, sympathy for a country's plight will not here ever issue in art, for back of it the impulse to art, to create an independent, durable object, a novel to survive the pretexts of its writing, is surely missing. Mr Aluko deplores the behaviour of his politicians, is in despair at their fandangling if sympathetic of their weaknesses, but this preoccupation is of a different kind from the reveries of creation. However Mr Aluko does catch very well the note of West African democratic politics: pacy, racy, brought by the exigencies of political manoeuvre into occasional clownishness, zestful of vulgar rhetoric:

> Nemesis has caught up with them, these plunderers of the wealth of the nation. They are now on the run, fleeing from the just anger of the electorate they have betrayed. They are now scurrying like rats, Ministers of State who used their positions of trust to build mansions for themselves and their girl friends.

Yet the novel is nevertheless fundamentally serious; we are well aware that political choice is not an affair of levity. And so *Chief the Honourable Minister* is remote from cynicism or despair: behind its scolding there is assurance of the possibilities of reform.

Fixions: I am too interested to know whether Mr Taban lo Liyong's manner, as an M.A. from the famous Writers Workshop of Iowa University, did or did not, in its unconventionality, please his Professors. His approach to his readers is at any rate a little that of a sardonic tease. He writes as it happens with considerable assurance. As **141** is only proper – and a matter of some relief – this assurance is an effect principally of intelligence in the writing, of some such agreeable thing being manifestly there to see. Only marginally is there that sense (huffily communicated) that difficulties, of obscurity, of intention, are in this day and age meetly to be resolved by the reader's himself having recourse, in his distress, to a Readers Workshop doubtless adjacently housed.

But what are 'Fixions'? I am unable to find the word in any dictionary at hand. Perhaps a punning compound is intended. For the story to which the title is attached is certainly about a 'fix': it deals with (in the modern African context) the topical theme of corruption and also with insurrection. Inordinately brief, summary and off-hand, it might, I suppose, be just a gesture, a fiction about a 'fix', hence 'fixion': the whimsy of the pun just about giving the note of the gesture.

A reminiscence in style of Tutuola is clear in many of the other eight pieces, one of which is dedicated to this writer, from whom, Mr Lyong intimates, he has learnt much, and most importantly, of the need for courage. The point is well-taken. I am almost inclined to go back to Tutuola and read him again, as with a sense of a style revivified. Perhaps it would turn out to be an illusion. The difference at any rate – weave hynotically though the bush-path of narrative will – is that Mr Liyong slips along it with a greater (and slyer) sense of route and destination. In Tutuola's position he must be rather more conscious of the need for courage. I should make it clear that he puts the style of obscure – or as one should say – obscured narrative principally to the purpose of mockery: the path necessarily weaves obscurely through the giant forest – a road, cut wide, straight and as it were lucidly, would after all run through' the forest in a different sense, with those conveyed swiftly along it now dissociated; it is, if what is wanted is the forest, bush-path or nothing. Hence Tutuola. Mr Liyong more or less slyly indicates this, but he is concerned, unlike his mentor, to jab: he gets his reader into the forest when he thought he was outside. Plenty of sympathy; and with traditional Africa. More art too perhaps, irony, after all one of its more honoured literary modes, being deftly deployed.

G. D. Killam:
The Novels of Chinua Achebe

Derek Elders

G. D. Killam, *The Novels of Chinua Achebe*, Heinemann, London, and Africana Publishing Corporation, New York, 1969.

If Dr Killam's monograph on Achebe's four novels is pedestrian in treatment and uninspiring in content it is not altogether his fault: responsible criticism can scarcely achieve a greater subtlety or interest than its material. African fiction still largely interests by its treatment of matters peripheral to the intrinsically literary: by what the works are about rather than what they are as works of art. Indeed, the book under review quotes Achebe's own suggestion that he writes 'applied art' and further quotations sufficiently indicate his didactic leanings. Soyinka is a rare example of an African writer who, with an eye for the telling detail, for the nuances of social behaviour, possesses the genuinely artistic gift for 'realisation', the ability to force a scene to come convincingly alive – consider the Oguazors' party in *The Interpreters*. However, it is Achebe who represents what might be called the central line of development ('tradition' would be altogether too portentous and premature a term) of Anglophone African fiction. It is essentially the line of anthropological reconstruction, a coming to terms with the past as a preparation for a closer look at a disquieting present; and, in terms of literature, a preparation for possible future achievement rather than achievement itself. It is a progress not without interest but the interest belongs to the phenomenon.

Not that these reflections deter Dr Killam who writes as one hastily fulfilling a brief to produce a book, possessing no qualms about the particular usefulness of the undertaking, and having a weekend conveniently free. Admittedly one could place this book in the hands of students without their coming to much harm, if little genuinely critical enlightenment. From this point of view it is a godsend when compared with, say, the 'Notes and Essays' on *Things Fall Apart* perpetrated by Messrs Adelusi and Adejumo on unsuspecting 'O' level candidates, and propagated by a firm of publishers who are undaunted by the implications of the word 'educational' which they prefix to their name – a pamphlet whose critical pretensions are heralded by such remarks as **143**

'The author depicts a high sense of literary ability by using various devices which have done great credit to the novel', and in which a gruesomely inconclusive battle is fought between the ineptitude of the writers and the incompetence of the compositors.

But – and here is the reason for the above apparently digressive comparison – whilst Dr Killam's book does not exhibit anything like the spectacular debasement of criticism to examination fodder represented by the 'Notes and Essays', it is arguable that it demonstrates a merely more sophisticated version of a common malaise in the criticism of African fiction; an unwillingness or inability to approach these works with anything like the integrity that academic expectations in an English or American context would demand and enforce. African literature, it ought to be admitted, cannot compete in depth and quality with the more established canons. This is by no means a gratuitous paternalism: given the conditions of its origins and development it is simply in the nature of the case. And an unfortunate corollary is that African literature is, with very rare exceptions, sold short by critical standards. Hypocritical praise or a fatuous application of analytic techniques whose sophistication is far in excess of the material they affect to elucidate does a grave disservice to the development of African writing – and one more pernicious than the well-intentioned obtuseness of the authors of 'Notes and Essays'.

This brings one by a gloomy circuitousness to a more particular consideration of the work under review. Dr Killam's method is to sandwich between an introduction and conclusion four chapters dealing with the four novels seen as a tetralogy revealing 'the extent to which traditional values have been turned upside down' to end 'in gloom and uncertainty'. However, Dr Killam makes it plain at the outset that he does not wish to add his voice to the mass of anthropological or political commentary which so often passes for the literary criticism of African fiction; but, rather, to focus his attention on 'the overall excellence of these books as pieces of fiction, as works of art'. It is a laudable, if perhaps unwittingly optimistic, intention. A reasonably sophisticated reader might well feel that the task is unnecessary, that a consideration of Achebe's novels as works of literary art requires no higher function than the reviewer's. And, in the event, the comments Dr Killam offers and the extracts he quotes as he conscientiously retails the plots of the four novels must have a drearily familiar ring to any teacher who has conducted a course in African fiction. There is after all only one set of things that any competent critic could possibly find to say about these novels – and much of the comment by way of explaining the unfamiliar. As a pedagogical exercise at this level the book is not without usefulness. But Dr Killam promises more: indeed he offers himself as a literary critic, a role inviting a closer scrutiny of credentials than that of the honest painstaking teacher.

From this point of view, his chapter on *Things Fall Apart* is the most interesting section of his book and it is also representative of the general method of approach. After his brief introduction which rehearses the by now familiar problems of cultural background, the linguistic situation, post-colonial disorientation – topics which have a livelier impact in the abundant quotation from Achebe himself than in Dr Killam's enveloping explanatory prose – he comes to *Things Fall Apart* as 'the first novel by a Nigerian writer to have serious claim to consideration as literature'. It is a claim indifferently served by the consideration it actually receives. For, having committed himself to serious literary criticism of the work on which Achebe's reputation principally rests, Dr Killam finds himself unable to say anything to the point. And, like others in this situation, he falls back on a labouring of the obvious or a self-deluding discussion of significances that are largely invented (the male and female principles in the novel being elevated to a symbolic importance somewhat in excess of their apparent contribution to the events of the plot). There are too many remarks which coyly hint at unrevealed beauties, subtleties too deep to be plumbed, nuances too fine to be exhibited. *Things Fall Apart* is hardly the novel to subdue critical confidence to a tentative reticence. On the contrary, this evasiveness is more likely to arise from a decent embarrassment, from the uneasy sense that one's critical poise, one's appearance of a respectable sophistication, can be tenuously maintained only by a guarded inexplicitness. Hence, on the real object of criticism – the actual handling of the language – Dr Killam finds himself gingerly prodding at the adequate if uninspiring crust of Achebe's prose style and darkly hinting at the unexpected plums he could produce had he a mind to. So, he commends to our attention writing that is 'apparently casual', a 'seeming simplicity of statement', a 'characteristic economy' which, he asserts manfully, 'belies' a 'complexity' which to those as unsubtle as the present writer remains obstinately opaque. In commenting on the 'deftness and certainty' of the novel's opening paragraphs Dr Killam assures us that:

> In extrapolating sentences out of context one often does an author a disservice. Full exegesis of the first chapter would reveal an even greater complexity of meaning and richness of texture in the prose.

Greater than what? And why the uneasy conditional? The unconvinced would perhaps be grateful for a little less plot-precis and rather more **145** explicit demonstration of these tantalisingly concealed delights. Ian Watt's explication of the first paragraph of *The Ambassadors* would place the present charade in a decisively dismissive context. The disservice lies not in extracting sentences but in critical charlatanism.

Dr Killam's endeavours to provide a critical framework for his discussion go further than undemonstrated claims of linguistic subtlety and draw him into generalisations that seem altogether too weighty for the occasion. One's sense here is not of particularities which find no critical endorsement of their alleged interest but rather a general feeling of inappropriateness. The effect of something having strayed in from another level of critical discourse may be explained by the fact that the remarks in question were anticipated – in both thought and phrasing – by Arnold Kettle's essay on *Wuthering Heights* where the context provided by that novel gives them the security of relevance.

The quite fundamental difficulty displayed in Dr Killam's book is that works in their literary infancy simply do not lend themselves to the habitual critical procedures of more developed literary situations. The critic can either admit that this is so – and pay the literature in question the compliment of honest appraisal – or he can, as Dr Killam attempts to do, conduct an elaborate pretence by implying the presence of standards which are perhaps inappropriate, perhaps untimely, and certainly not met. To pretend that they are met is to falsify the object of criticism or – worse, from the point of view of its future growth – to expose it to the ridicule of the sophisticated.

The critic's uncertainty about the status of his material is evident in various remarks in his introduction. Presenting Achebe as having a claim to be 'a novelist in the fullest sense of the word', Dr Killam observes:

> More recent comment on Achebe has sought to relate him to the literary traditions of England. This is appropriate since not only does he write in English and prefer to be judged by the general critical standards which apply, but also he admits that the writers who have influenced him number among them Conrad, Graham Greene, Waugh and others, and thus it would be expected that his work would fit into the general pattern of English fiction in the twentieth century. To suggest the general literary milieu into which Achebe's work may be placed is to suggest a critical context for examining his work. It does not, however, account for the excellence of the writing.

The problems involved in finding an appropriate manner of approach to African fiction, raised here, are of basic importance and urgently need critical discussion; but they cannot be adequately engaged with by vaguely invoking 'the general critical standards which apply' in a literary milieu' which, albeit with Achebe's prompting, can assimilate both Conrad and Graham Greene. It is tempting to say that:

> In accepting a world language as a medium of literary exchange, African novelists suggest a criterion by which they would wish their work to be judged.

But Dr Killam realises that the problem is not solved that easily:

> African writers are faced with difficulties not usually encountered by novelists writing in a world language, in this case English. They are in an important sense outside the literary traditions of England.

One's complaint, however, is that in his actual practice Dr Killam ignores the problems he implies here and can work from such naïve standards as the following in the chapter on *Arrow of God:*

> Achebe's indication of his intention as explained here provides a basis for judging the book and a point of view from which it may be judged.

The real issue is not the explicit definition of standards but the nature and quality of the standards implied in a particular critical response to particular local effects. In Dr Killam's critical practice, the advertised excellence of Achebe's writing practically becomes its own criterion. His remarks never get much further than to find Achebe's language appropriate to his themes and to deck out competent plot summaries – largely composed of direct quotations whose intrinsic interest scarcely justifies their length or their frequency – with a small arsenal of dignifying phrases and a nominal bow to critical discrimination in allowing *No Longer at Ease* to have a 'minor flaw'.

Dr Killam's book is offered as a 'commentary' for those who 'have felt the need for straightforward and enlightened guidance' and which 'will answer the needs of universities and schools'.

A Curse From God
By Stephen Ngubiah

Bahadur Tejani

Stephen Ngubiah. *A Curse from God*, East African Literature Bureau, Nairobi.

In publishing this novel, both the writer and the East African Literature Bureau have undertaken a bold risk, as it is one of the very few coldly logical viewpoints on the African past. Mr Ngubiah's problem is strictly local, his roots definitely East African and his audience specifically African. For the writer it is the choice between polygamy and monogamy, the traditional Gikuyu and the neo-Christian values, that tears apart the life of Karagu, the central character. The writer is decisively pro-Christian, for monogamy and against tradition. In this he is the very antithesis of Ngugi and Okot and more recently the neo-romance of Kimbhugwe and mother-admiration of Kibera. Ngubiah's viewpoint necessarily diversifies and enriches the artistic world around us. Here we find Karagu the father looking at the scene around his hut, through the author's eyes.

'The children kept on chasing one another, passing in front of their father every few seconds. He found himself counting their skeletal bodies, as they passed him. All were eleven; eleven long-necked, sickly, pot-bellied, emaciated individuals. A great compassion seized him. He wished it were in his power to change their wretched condition.'

But the irony of the situation speaks for itself in the continuing paragraph as the second wife emerges from her hut.

'Muthoni came out with a chair and sat leaning against a wall a short distance from him [Karagu]. Her big protruding stomach, heavy with child, hung heavily between her knees, its weight straining and flattening the muscles of the neck and face; giving them a gaunt and bony appearance. A dismayed look tinged her eyes, and her face displayed a fatigued expression.'

As it happens the delivery yields twins and in the next paragraph, after Muthoni has returned from a caesarian section at the hospital, the writer adds grim humour to the situation.

'Three years is considered too long a time for a woman to stay without a baby. When Muthoni stayed for three years and did not have a new baby, she began to get worried.' So after consultation with Wacu the witchdoctor, she forces her husband, whilst denying him sexual entry, to give him money to remove the spells and beget more children.

With such a superstitious second wife, fourteen children, no land, and rejection of Christian tradition of sobriety and self-control, Karagu becomes a *Kinuya Mai*, or the Big Boozer. To emphasise his point, the writer turns him into a sexual Frankenstein, a woman-hitter, and child-murderer, who finally takes his own life.

Just before Karagu's death, the following emotions are seen running through his mind.

'He surveyed his wherabouts for the last time. The river ran from West to East and on either side of it lay each of the two lands: One his and the other Wanjiru's sons' land [his first wife]. He was the river and his wives were the two ridges. Two wives one man and the vice-versa was an impracticable venture. It occurred to him that his body dangling on that tree would symbolise a factor which would keep his home divided, like a *Gitoka*, Amaryllis lily which the Gikuyu use to mark their land boundaries.'

The divisions in family life are very well-captured, when Karagu marries a second wife. The quarrels between Wanjiru and Muthoni range from fights over soap, food and harvesting, to accusations of witchcraft and theft. The violence, the hate, the betrayals by father of children and by son of father, are rendered vividly and frighteningly.

Natural forces like famine and political forces like the repression of the Gikuyu by the English are used to create a largeness of effect. It seems that the whole of the cosmic order has combined to persecute the main character, as if he has been cursed by God. His dilemma, frustration, and degeneration are done objectively without much sympathy, with understanding, and with an eye on the future. Ngubiah stands for a more controlled and balanced view of life. For him, this inevitably includes monogamy and the rest of the pro-Christian modern values which go with it.

At times the book suffers from monotony. Since this is the author's first novel and we expect more from his pen, it is necessary to point out that a great deal of the conversation between the father, his wives and sons, and among the neighbours, is carried on in the same style and needs variation. Too often the characters are shown to be 'blurting', 'spurting', 'blaring' or 'spitting hotly'. Their reactions are predictable, though this a part of the author's design.

149

It should also be pointed out that his portrayal of the Asian characters and background is stereotype and without imagination. The District
Commissioner, Mr Fox, suffers the same treatment. The author makes
out that the Singhs speak Gujerati at home, whereas the Sikh language
is Punjabi. He also tries to put the following conversation pieces in their
mouths, to demonstrate their illiteracy, which is illogical since most
of the East African Asians were literate before the East African Africans. Mr Singh is given the following remarks: 'My wife you show work
okay?' 'You ask why?' 'What wrong to wash them?' 'All clothes wash
you, and no trouble here you make. Okay?' In comparison with which
Karugu who is only a KAPE speaks faultless English. Nor is there any
consistency in the kind of English Ngubiah assumes his Punjabi characters to be using.

Idu
Flora Nwapa

Adeola A. James

Flora Nwapa, *Idu*, Heinemann, 1969.

In *Idu* the writer tries to dramatise the importance of children in an
African marriage, or the value that Africans attach to children. To
portray this theme we watch the dramas in the lives of two different
women – these are Idu the heroine and Ojiugo who is described as Idu's
great friend. Flora Nwapa tends to idealise her heroines, as is apparent
from both her earlier novel *Efuru* and this recent one. In this new novel,
Idu is presented as the picture of a perfect woman, an ideal wife, industrious, kind-hearted and loving. She is also a friendly and hospitable
woman who is loved and respected by everyone in her community. The
only blemish in her life is that she is childless, and although her husband
Adiewere is unusual in that he is not particularly disturbed about this,
Idu herself spends hours weeping over her misfortune. Eventually,
after several instigations and persuasions from various quarters she
finds a young wife for her husband. This action disturbs the tranquillity
of Idu's and Adiewere's married life because the nameless girl, often
referred to as 'the small wife' does not fit into their pattern of life. But
150 this episode falls short of being a disaster because Idu herself becomes

pregnant and gives birth to Ijoma, and the young wife, of her own accord, leaves and marries another man. Idu and Adiewere's life continues in the same peaceful way and it is much enriched with the arrival of Ijoma who is regarded as a prodigy in many ways, especially as he was born on a day on which there was an eclipse of the sun.

Another illustration of the theme previously stated – the importance of children in an African marriage – is Ojiugo and Amarajeme's marriage. Ojiugo, like Idu, is industrious and has all the qualities of a good woman. As a result of her ways her husband worships her. But their marriage is also childless and Ojiugo one day disappears having confided in her friend Idu that she is going to live with Obukodi, her husband's friend, who is the father of her expected child.

Both marriages, in fact, end tragically: Ojiugo's husband Amarajeme hangs himself when he learns that Ojiugo has a son. In Idu's case, the pattern of her calm, happy married life continues for some time. Her brief anxiety over having another child is also dispelled when in Ijoma's fourth year Idu finds that she is going to have another baby. Then Adiewere mysteriously dies. Idu flouts all conventions by refusing to marry her husband's brother, and dies shortly afterwards out of grief.

This, briefly, is the totality of the action dramatised in *Idu*. In spite of its potentially significant theme, the novel fails to grip; it leaves the reader cold and uninvolved. This is because of two serious faults in the writer's handling of her narrative and her attitude to her story.

I consider the theme of the novel, as stated above, potentially significant because it is a theme that can be used to question the dominant attitude among Africans to children as the basic if not the only reason for marriage. This attitude often leads to dissolution of a childless marriage and sometimes to graver consequences. But Flora Nwapa fails to realise the potentiality of her theme because she has not ventured beyond a prosaic narrative statement of the situation as it is. This failure becomes more serious when one considers that she manifests a similar weakness in *Efuru*, her first novel, which also like *Idu* attempts to dramatise a potentially serious theme – that of man's complex relationship with the gods – where again at the end of the novel one is not only unmoved, but is also not certain about the aim of the novel.

Unlike other writers who use the traditional societies of Africa as a background, Flora Nwapa shows no moral involvement in the realities behind her tale. Her novels would be more successful if she could involve the reader by first involving herself in the deep moral problems which she mentions, but leaves unquestioned.

The second serious fault of this novel is in its thematic uncertainty. The theme as illustrated in the lives of Idu and Ojiugo is clearly stated **151** by one of the characters who, sympathising with Idu, says 'What we are all praying for is children. What else do we want if we have children?' But certainly later events in the novel do not bear out this theme. For both women, in spite of having children, still refuse to live on after the deaths of their respective husbands. In Idu's words Ojiugo 'died' the day that her husband Amarajeme died. Idu's case is even more puzzling for she knows she is pregnant when Adiewere dies but she still insists on joining him, as her words prove: 'I have not forgotten Ijoma, my son. And the one in my womb . . . I will have it in the land of the dead.' Not long after this statement her wishes are fulfilled. This surely is another example of a clear dissociation between the writer's intention and her realisation.

Apart from these two fundamental weaknesses, one is dissatisfied with the total effect of the novel. On putting the book aside after reading it, there are hardly any memorable incidents one can recall, because the bulk of the story is made up of bits of gossip instead of interaction of characters. Even the few incidents one can recall such as Idu's death and Amarajeme's suicide suffer from serious flaws. The effect of Amarajeme's suicide is pathos, not tragedy. Although the words chosen to describe Amarajeme's taking of his own life by hanging and its aftermath do echo Okonkwo's tragic end in *Things Fall Apart*, yet here the highly emotive words fall flat and seem misplaced essentially because Amarajeme is not a convincing character. He does not behave like a man, he seems morally weak rather than doomed, therefore his end does not arouse in us the pity and fear necessary for a tragic experience.

In the case of Idu's death our moral perspective remains equivocal because of the writer's own lack of moral involvement. Are we to regard Idu's final rejection of life and children in preference to following her dead husband as a courageous act, or is it an indication of the deepest kind of love, or is it a cowardly act – a failure to face up to the responsibilities of motherhood? This is not the type of ambivalence which arises from depth of understanding and therefore leaves the reader with a rich and complex experience. One feels rather that it is a confused statement essentially due to the writer's failure to explore to its fullest the possibilities of her story.

Considering her performances in both *Efuru* and *Idu* one cannot help wondering what motivates Miss Nwapa beyond the elementary wish of everyone to be a writer. In her novels there is a complete absence of that phenomenon that has been described by various writers as the impulse to write which 'kicks you in the pit of your stomach'. If this impulse is absent one expects, at least, to be compensated by other things such as beautiful narrative style, amusing and vividly described incidents and powerful characterisation. All these are sadly missing in both *Efuru* and *Idu*.

The Nigerian and Cameroonian Novel

Willfried Feuser

Otto Bischofberger, *Tradition und Wandel aus der Sicht der Roman-schriftsteller Kameruns und Nigerias*, Neue Zeitschrift für Missions-wissenschaft. Schöneck-Beckenreid (Switzerland), 1968.

'The phenomenon of literature cannot be reduced to social meanings.' Heeding this warning by Albert Nemmi, the Tunisian writer and socio-logist, and encouraged by Cyprian Ekwensi, Otto Bischofberger here attempts a contrastive sociological analysis of the Cameroonian and Nigerian novel. His attention is mainly focused on the dynamics of tradition and cultural change.

It is not an easy task to align the four Cameroonian novelists – Beti, Oyono, Matip, and Ikellé-Matiba – in such a way as to balance the ever-growing group of Nigerian writers, of whom a total of eleven is dis-cussed. The author takes great pains trying to explain the respective distribution of the two literatures in time. Both started in the early 'fifties but while the Cameroons, after Beti's and Oyono's spirited and accomplished outbursts during the second half of the decade, seem to have sunk all of a sudden into a state of almost total torpor, Nigeria's curve of creative writing has kept rising steadily and has hardly shown any signs of fatigue after independence. Dr Bischofberger sees the reason for the Cameroons' lack of literary impetus during the post-independence period in the fact that writers like Beti and Oyono were radically committed to the anti-colonial struggle. When the cause of irritation was removed, or felt to be removed, they suddenly found themselves without a worthwhile area of attack. The young bulls trotted out of the arena for lack of a red cloth.

The attitude of the Cameroonian novelist towards tradition is **153** ambivalent; his links with the past are tenuous. A strong sense of alienation from his society, brought about by two successive modes of assimilation policy – German and French – led to violent reactions against the *colonisateur* as well as the product of his endeavours, the *colonisé*.

The Nigerian authors felt the impact of colonisation far less directly. Tradition was not as overtly disrupted under their own eyes. Though the same agents of change – the missionaries and administrators – were at work in Nigeria, theirs was a different tempo and a different style. The Nigerian writer has therefore always felt free to re-create and re-interpret his tradition.

He may be haunted by it like Tutuola, he may make a conscious and coherent attempt at ancestor-worship like Achebe, or like Soyinka he may occasionally protest against its encroachment on the present as 'the existing fossil within society, the dead branches on a living tree, the dead runs on the bole' – the Nigerian writer is always on familiar terms with his tradition; it is part and parcel of an unselfconscious 'cultural' nationalism. The Cameroonian writer's nationalism, though more pronounced, is in the main 'politically' inclined. His is a literature of anti-colonial protest; he may attempt a wistful return to the past, as Mongo Beti does in his *Mission to Kala*, but it ends in disillusionment, and the hero joins the uprooted mass of humanity in a faceless and nameless city. His forlornness, one might say, is symbolic of the crisis into which post-independence literature in the Cameroons, and to a large extent in the whole French-speaking West Africa, has fallen, although there are now signs of a new awakening.

Dr Bischofberger has marshalled a wealth of material along the two axes of tradition and change. He draws upon numerous background studies, among them Belgian and Cameroonian journals and German dissertations with a missionary bias which are hard to come by in any West African library. Taking recognised authorities in the field such as Balandier and Alexandre as his lode-stars, he manages to maintain a reasonable standard of impartiality throughout, although his own point of view would seem to be rather anaemic, especially in the first half of the book. Nevertheless neither the social anthropologist nor the student of African literature aiming at a socially relevant evaluation of the Cameroonian and Nigerian novel can afford to by-pass this work.

Index